GOON
FOR LUNCH

Also by Harry Secombe
TWICE BRIGHTLY

GOON FOR LUNCH

Harry Secombe

M. and J. Hobbs
in association with
Michael Joseph

First published in Great Britain by
M. and J. HOBBS
25 Bridge Street, Walton-on-Thames
in association with
MICHAEL JOSEPH LTD
52 Bedford Square, London W.C.1
1975
Second impression before publication

ISBN 0 7181 1283 0

Printed and bound in Great Britain by
REDWOOD BURN LIMITED
Trowbridge & Esher

To my wife and family
who bear the pangs of authorship
with great fortitude

The author wishes to thank the Editor and Proprietors of the following magazines for permission to reproduce material which originally appeared in their pages.

The Broken Spectacles, Needle Match and The Wedding – *Argosy;* A Bomb in the Bed – *Evening News;* Bright is Right, Busy Doing Nothing, God and Dai, Goon for Lunch, Idiot on Parade, Middle-aged Man and the Sea, In Praise of Corn, The Scars of Summer, Summertime and the Living is Easy, That Christmas and Elsie, To be Honest and Which is the Way to the Crocodiles? – *Punch;* Milligan's Overcoat and A Night in a Cell – *Sunday Citizen;* Fireworks in July – *The Times.* Also Cassel & Co. for Goon Away which first appeared – *The Twelfth Man.*

The author wishes to thank himself for contributing the illustrations to this book.

CONTENTS

FOREWORD

These stories are mostly apochryphal, although I will not pretend that there is more than a grain of truth in all of them. I am not going to say, therefore, that all the characters in them bear no resemblance to anyone in real life.

I would like to dedicate this book to all those people with whom I grew up, served in the Army and worked in the theatre. They are all in here in one form or another and I thank them for providing me with such a wealth of material.

I The Wedding

It was a hot Saturday afternoon in July, and Billy Evans and Kenny Thomas and the gang had gone up Kilvey Hill to look for tadpoles. I was in my 'delicate' phase at the time, after having had a series of childhood illnesses one after the other. I had measles so quickly on top of chicken pox that the spots were fighting each other for space. Now I was getting over jaundice and was only allowed out near the house.

When Joyce Llewellyn came over to me I was reading a book of poetry by Keats which my grandfather had given me. Somehow I felt a kinship with the delicate poet and had also taken to leaping around the front room improvising ballet steps to the music on the radio, whilst my parents exchanged vaguely worried glances. You might say that I was positively ethereal at this time.

'Come on, Harry,' said Joyce, showering me with spit. 'We're playing weddings and you're the bridegroom.'

I looked up startled.

'I've been ill,' I said timorously, knowing the rigours of Joyce's games. 'Besides, my mother says I'm only to play near the front door.'

She tried another tactic.

'Mildred will be awful upset,' she said. 'She's the bride.'

My head swam, and the book dropped from my lap. Mildred Reilly – the girl I worshipped from afar, the girl with the Shirley Temple dimples, the girl whose 'Hello' could send me into a decline. She was a newcomer to the district and her parents only let her play with us very occasionally. Her dad had a three-wheeled Morgan run-

10

about, in the back of which she sat like a little princess, as they chugged down St Leger Crescent on their regular Sunday outing.

I had caught a chill one Sunday evening waiting in the rain for the car to come home so that I could just see her wave to me. She didn't wave either, she was asleep in her mother's arms. If I could have thought of a rhyme for 'Mildred' I would have written a poem about her.

Joyce was irritated. 'Are you coming or not? Tom Williams is over by there – I'll ask him then.'

I was at her side in two strides as she turned away. 'All right then,' I said, my voice high-pitched and trembly. 'If it's Mildred, I don't mind.'

'I thought you wouldn't,' said Joyce with an old-fashioned look.

We went across to the Patch where the ceremony was to be performed. This 'patch' was a square-shaped piece of waste ground which lay helplessly in the middle of our little community of council houses, as if the architect had left a packet of cigarettes on the blueprint and had absent-mindedly worked around it. All the windows of the houses around faced on to it, so parents would keep an eye on we kids who had made it our playground.

They had set up a tent made from blankets and an old eiderdown with two broomsticks as the central supports, and a group of chattering girls stood outside it. As we came near, one of them squealed 'He's coming, Mildred – get back in quick. He musn't see you before you marry him.' There was a giggle and a flash of pink and the blanket in front of the tent was secured with a large safety pin.

Joyce poked around on the ground in a heap of clothes. 'Here try these on,' she said, throwing me a pair of striped pants.

Red-faced, my glasses steamed with perspiration I struggled into them. Jessie Probert snickered slyly. 'Aren't you going to take your other pants off first then?' She was a big girl for her age.

I stood upright, clutching the trousers at the waist to keep them up. 'They're a bit too big,' I stammered, embarrassed and a little frightened by the proximity of so many girls with no other boy for moral support.

Joyce Llewellyn regarded me critically. She was now wearing her idea of a parson's outfit, with her father's stiff collar back to front and a homburg hat rammed down over her stringy red hair. She bent down and picked up a length of string from amongst the heap of clothing. Her father was a sailor and the way she trussed me around the waist would have made him a proud man.

'There now, that'll hold 'em,' she remarked with satisfaction.

I fought for breath against the stricture of her reef knots. 'Don't you think you tied it too tight,' I gasped.

'Nonsense, you can't have 'em falling down during the ceremony, and besides you've gone a much better colour,' my Torquemada replied.

I stood helplessly, near to tears, and wishing I had never been tempted into coming along.

A coat was flung at me. 'Try that for size,' spat Joyce.

I tried it on defeatedly to find that it was a tail coat which enveloped me in all directions, but before I could take it off again Joyce called, 'Are you ready Harry – Mildred's getting impatient, her mother's coming home from shopping soon.'

At the mention of Mildred's name, I melted. To be near her, to hold her hand would be worth all this dressing up.

I submitted meekly to being led into position outside the tent, where the girls had set up an old packing case as an altar. Joyce stood in front of me with a tattered copy of *Pears Cyclopaedia* in her hands and behind me the other girls, acting as bridesmaids, started to sing 'Here comes the Bride' in three different keys.

I could feel the hair rising on the back of my neck as I heard her footsteps behind me. She stopped beside me, and I turned round as far as my string belt would allow to look at her.

Her dress was long and pink and full of holes. Her hat was a cloche-type hat belonging to her mother, her lips were made up with lip-stick which had smudged and she was wearing high heeled shoes several sizes too big. To me she was the most beautiful creature I had ever seen.

When she put her hand on my arm, I shook like a leaf and I vowed silently that I would die for her; I would fight all the dragons in the world for her; I would see that she had ice cream every day and she would never have to go to school if she didn't want to.

'Do you take this woman to be your lawful wedded wife?' intoned Joyce from a page of *Pears Cyclopaedia*.

I nodded dumbly. 'Say "I do",' hissed the 'parson'.

'I do,' came croaking from my throat.

'Do you take this man to be your – err – lawfully wedded husband?'

'I do,' lisped my beloved through the gaps in her front teeth.

'Where's the ring?' spat Joyce.

'Here it is,' cried Jessie Probert, dropping her end of Mildred's frock and rushing forward with a gold ring.

'Be careful, it's my Mam's and she'll kill me if she finds I've pinched it.'

'Put it on her finger,' I was commanded.

Taking her hot sticky little hand in mine I placed the ring on her finger where it dangled loosely. My heart was full and the rest of the ceremony was lost in a welter of happiness.

'I now pronounce you man and wife,' declared Joyce Llewellyn in a spray of triumphant spittle, shutting the book firmly.

'Kiss the bride,' she said.

Mildred lifted her cheek demurely and with all the tenderness in my young world I kissed her.

'You're sweating,' said the girl who held my heart in her hands and she rubbed her cheek vigorously where I had kissed it.

'Open the bottle of pop and get them broken biscuits' – Joyce was on the job again. 'Let's have the reception.'

'Let's have some then,' said my bride leaving my side with an alacrity that hurt. All the other girls crowded around her giggling and chattering leaving me bewildered and alone. They all crowded into the tent after the pop and biscuits. I stood uncertainly outside, feeling suddenly much older. Then Mildred came out and offered me a drink from her cup.

'Use the other side,' she said 'I've got lipstick on.'

Gratefully I accepted, not realising how thirsty I was, and before I had realised it I had drained the cup.

'You greedy thing,' she cried. 'You're only supposed to take a sip.' She slapped my face. 'I hate you. Old four eyes – old yellow face,' she chanted, turning the knife in the wound. 'You look awful silly in those clothes,' and turning on her heel she went back into the tent.

I couldn't see for tears. I stood biting my lip. 'I've been ill,' I blubbed through the opening in the tent. Her back was turned to me and the other girls all giggled as I stuck my head inside.

'You wait,' I began, then hearing footsteps behind me I saw Billy Evans and Kenny Thomas with jars full of tadpoles in their hands.

'Look what we got,' said Billy holding his jam pot in the air. 'There's about two thousand tadpoles in there at least.'

Then seeing my strange get-up Kenny Thomes said, 'What are you doing? You've been playing with the girls.'

'I haven't,' I said. 'Well, anyway, I didn't want to – it's all Joyce Llewellyn's fault.'

'Let's knock their tent down,' said Billy Evans kicking at the broomstick supporting the back of it.

The girls shouted angrily inside as we pushed the tent over, and Joyce Llewellyn pummelled all three of us as we pulled the blankets over their heads.

'You've spoiled the reception, you've ruined everything,' she cried hysterically, tears streaming down her face.

Mildred, my Mildred, ran sobbing to her house as I shouted, 'Serves you right, serves you right,' with a throat constricted with hatred and love all mixed up together.

Then my mother came out and called me in, and I went to bed early. I didn't have any supper, not because I was refused it, but because I didn't feel like it.

But I had a good breakfast on Sunday morning. It was laver bread and bacon and fried potatoes and when I saw Mildred Reilly next I stuck my tongue out at her.

I finished with Keats, too – I think I was starting to grow up, or something.

2   The Kindly Conspiracy

It was one of those warm hazy summer mornings that only occur in childhood. Kenny Thomas and I sat on his mother's back doorstep looking out at the Swansea Docks across the wild triangle of blackcurrant bushes and runner bean sticks that represented the Proberts's garden, contemplating on how to spend the day.

The council house back gardens stretched down the hill before us in a patchwork revelation of individual horticultural prowess. The sunflowers in the Williams's family plot which reached proudly towards their bedroom windows were the result of an accidentally spilled packet of seeds, whilst at number 7, Leger Crescent the Dentons's petunias and peonies grew in the disciplined rows which ex-Sgt. Major Denton (Welsh Guards) ordained for them from the moment he had made his choice from Carter's mail order catalogue.

Cats prowled the wilderness of his next door neighbours, the Llewellyn's backyard, like miniature tigers on some Indian game reserve, occasionally making forays into the drilled plantations of the ex-Army gardener who stood constant watch over his well-ordered domain from his bedroom window, permanently perched on a spring mattress howdah, a Daisy air rifle across his withered shanks. His only victim in the past three months had been a large ginger tom cat who seemed to belong to no one in particular. He had shot it in the act of copulation with a half-Persian from the Vicarage. It was on record that the recipient of the pellet paused only briefly before finishing what it had begun and that it limped away into the shelter

18

of the Llewellyn's scabrous weeds with a backward glance of fine disdain towards his assailant's window. This brought a spatter of applause from other bedroom window occupants who were glad to have a diversion from watching St Thomas's first eleven being annihilated by a scratch side from the Seamen's Mission on the 65-degree slope cricket pitch which bordered the gardens.

Today, though, all was quiet on the agricultural front, and only the desultory siren of a banana boat disturbed the calm of the pristine day.

'Hless go for a hwalk up to the rezzer on Hilvey Hill,' said my companion. This I immediately interpreted as 'Let's go for a walk up to the reservoir on Kilvey Hill'. Kenny had been born with a cleft palate which made his speech difficult for other people to understand. As his constant friend from the age of three I was the only one who could make out what he was saying. Even his parents had trouble. Whenever he was sent on a shopping errand by his mother I always had to go with him so that I could surreptitiously explain what he wanted. It was customary for him to make his order to the shopkeeper who would watch my lips while pretending to listen to Kenny. A kindly conspiracy in which all the local tradespeople shared.

'It's too hot to walk up the hill,' I said, my eyes on Jessie Probert who had emerged from her back door wearing her mother's tablecloth as a sarong. She was topless, but at ten years of age that was of no consequence. Jessie swayed up to the wire separating the two gardens and undulated her hips suggestively.

'I seen Dorothy Lamour last night in *Hurricane*,' she said. 'Let's play sailors and natives.'

'No thanks,' we said in unison. Jessie was a potential source of trouble – always wanting to play games which invariably ended in 'I'll show you mine if you'll show me yours'.

She stuck out her tongue and swayed off towards the Williams's fence where the head of Tom Williams was just visible amongst the sunflowers. He was two years older than we were and had more to show for it.

· Kenny and I breathed a collective sigh of relief and settled back on the step. I narrowed my eyes deliberately and pretended that I was in Africa. *Trader Horn* had played our local flea pit three months before and we were both hooked on the African jungle. The bean sticks and black-currant bushes looked like dense forest if one had enough imagination and God knows I had plenty. I caught the swish of a tail in the undergrowth and I was off on the trail of a lion.

'Try squinting up your eyes and pretending the Proberts's garden's like the jungle,' I said to Kenny. 'Look at that lion hiding up in the bush waiting to make the kill.' I pointed to the cat's tail waving amongst the leaves next door.

'Oh yeagh.' Kenny peered uncertainly in a different direction.

'Come on, you two,' said Mrs Thomas behind us. 'Go and get some meat from the butcher's.' She was a little plump woman who always smelt of apples and the sly hint of gin. By nature a pleasant person, she was however given to fits of sudden rage, the legacy of having for a husband a docker whose meal timetable did not always coincide with opening hours.

We stood up reluctantly. Kenny, in search of my imaginary lion's tail, had spotted something far more interesting and just as primeval in the antics of Jessie Probert and Tom Williams dimly seen through the screen of sun-flowers and blackcurrants.

'I want a quarter of a pound of steak and a half a pound of sausages,' said Mrs Thomas. 'On the book,' she added quickly.

We repeated the order together.

'That's right, good boys.' She looked at me with her eye-brows raised and I nodded slightly to let her know that I had the message right. 'Here's a penny each for going.'

This was an unexpected bonus and we clutched the coins gleefully as she took them from her apron pocket and placed them in our outstretched palms.

We made a bee-line across the Patch to Mrs Morris's, a widow who kept a sweet shop in the front parlour of her council house. It was illegal, but the rent man turned a blind eye to the fact out of compassion and a sweet tooth. The choice was agonising. For a penny we could have a quarter of Sharp's toffees or a lucky packet, which usually contained a liquorice root, transfers to stick on the back of your hand, some tiger nuts, a couple of sweet cigarettes and sherbet suckers. There were also pear drops, gob stoppers which changed colour as you sucked them, and an assortment of chocolate bars.

Eventually after much consultation while Mrs Morris, in a cross-over pinny and carpet slippers, waited patiently for our decision I settled for a lucky packet and Kenny pointed to the glass jar of pear drops. She handed me my purchase and, making a cone from a torn piece of the *South Wales Evening Post,* she dropped in it a half dozen of the pink and white sweets, hesitated half a second, looked at Kenny's upturned face, and added another two. Our pennies were duly passed over and, the complicated transaction completed, she put them into a little tin cash box on the mantelpiece. I thanked her on behalf of myself and my friend, who was incapable of doing so himself, having further complicated his speech defect with a mouthful of pear drops.

Outside in the street I examined my lucky packet. Beside the usual contents there was a small green tin frog which made a clicking noise when a tab of metal underneath it was pressed, and a strange looking object which appeared to be a twig. I put the transfers in my pocket for later use – I needed a saucer of water and infinite patience to get a perfect picture on the back of my hand. I would also get the back of my father's hand if he found me doing it. The sherbet sweets I disposed of by putting them in my mouth, and clicking the frog in rhythm with my chewing we sauntered contentedly down St Leger Crescent.

By the time we had got as far as Mrs Evans the Pop, a lady who sold flagons of a home-made brew without which no Sunday dinner was complete, and which had a tendency to explode if kept too long, Kenny was on the last of his pear drops and was trying to make it last as long as possible by taking it out of his mouth and licking it between his fingers. I was down to the twig which I was loth to try, but I had been brought up not to waste anything. I stopped by Mrs Evans's gate and licked it tentatively. It had a funny bitter-sweet taste which I had never before encountered. I closed my eyes and chewed a small piece, rolling it around on the tongue in the true tradition of the connoisseur. When I opened my eyes again, still unable to identify the taste, I found myself being observed through the dusty privet hedge. The ginger tom cat which belonged to no one lay in the shade watching me with slitted amber eyes, tail swishing. I backed away nervously. In my daydreams I would fearlessly stalk the African jungle in search of dangerous game, but in real life I had a great respect for all animals, having been kicked by a cow in Cardigan on holiday.

I stretched out my hand towards it in a protective gesture. It was the hand that held the twig, and the battered head came forward to sniff it. The smell seemed to please the cat and it took the twig in its mouth.

'Hless go,' said Kenny nervously. We were both aware of the animal's reputation for wildness and the two intrepid African explorers beat a hasty retreat.

We slowed up as we got to the bottom of the street, looked at each other and began laughing.

'Bang. Bang!' I shouted, clicking my tin frog. 'Fancy being afraid of a cat.'

'Yeagh,' smiled Kenny, his lips pink.

'You look like a girl with lipstick on,' I said. I made him look in the window of the Co-op. We fell about laughing again.

It was when we got to the ironmonger's that I had the feeling that I was being followed. I turned around and there behind me was the ginger tom cat. Its face bore as near an expression of bliss as it could muster and it wrapped itself around my legs, purring and licking its lips. In cat terms this was tantamount to the conversion of St Paul on the road to Damascus. But this was Port Tennant Road and led to Neath and I had not been aware of any blinding light. Then it dawned on Kenny and me that it must have been the twig from the lucky packet. To this day I have no idea what it was, but the effect on the cat was incredible. I could not shake it off and it walked alongside me all the way to the butcher's. When Kenny tried to smooth it, its claws came out and it growled a warning, but I could have kicked it up the street and it would have come back for more. I know, I tried it.

The butcher's shop was next door but one to an undertaker's and my mother never became a customer there for that reason. 'It's not nice,' she would say. The legend 'Family Butcher' in raised whited letters on the window coupled with its proximity to the funeral parlour used to put bizarre thoughts in my mind. I imagined rows of families, neatly butchered, hanging on hooks in his refrigerator, and the pig's head on display in the window with a tomato in its mouth looked too much like the late Mr Howells for comfort.

We went into the shop together, the three of us, the cat

firmly wedging itself between my legs. Before we could give our order in unison, the butcher's large wife, who sat by the cash register, shouted 'Get that cat out of here.' Her husband, in a straw hat and striped apron, nodded in agreement and sharpened his knife a little faster.

'It won't leave us,' I said.

'He's not serving you with that thing in here.'

Her husband nodded again.

I was in a terrible dilemma. Unless I was there to translate the order, Kenny might finish up with anything, and at the same time we would never get served if I stayed in the shop because the cat would not leave without me.

Meanwhile, Kenny, who had never been aware of the fact that I was the one who really did the messages for his mother, could not understand what I was getting excited about.

'Htake hthe hcat outhide,' he said calmly. 'HI'll hget hthe horder.'

'Get that bloody cat out.' The butcher's wife was getting hysterical.

I picked the cat up and left the shop with a heavy heart. They wouldn't even let me stand in the doorway and I stood out of sight in the undertaker's doorway with the cat kneading my chest with its claws through my short-sleeved celanese shirt.

Kenny came out a few minutes later.

'What did you get?' I said anxiously.

'Hsteak hand hsauhage.' He was beginning to think I was going potty.

I breathed a sigh of relief which ruffled the fur on the cat's face and sent it into fresh ecstasy.

'Oh, gerroff.' I detached its claws from my shirt and threw the cat roughly to the ground.

We got back to Kenny's mother's just as the church clock struck half past twelve. She was on her way up the stairs as

we came in through the kitchen door followed by the ginger
tom. Kenny proudly handed over the newspaper-wrapped
parcel.

'There's good boys,' she said.

I stood waiting anxiously as she unfolded the bundle. I
knew that Kenny had ordered steak and sausages and a
cautious feel had confirmed that he had got what he had
asked for. The important question was the amount he had
ordered. The difference between ordering a quarter of a
pound of steak and a half a pound of sausages, and a *half*
a pound of steak and a quarter of a pound of sausages
could upset the family budget for a week.

Mrs Thomas's smile faded as she saw what we had
bought. One of her sudden rages shook her and before she
spoke I knew that my suspicions had been confirmed.

'Half a pound of steak!' she screamed, weighing it
physically in her hand, and mentally in her mind against
the half bottle of gin the extra quarter of a pound represented. 'Who do you think I am, Mrs Rothschild?' As
she delivered this line, she hurled the steak from her in a
fine theatrical gesture. Kenny ducked, I swerved, and it hit
the rent man, who had just appeared in the doorway, in
the chest.

It fell to the floor and we all stood still like a waxwork
tableau. All, that is, except the ginger tom who, with that
lightning change of mood to which all cats are prone, trans-
ferred its affection from me to the steak and in a blur of
movement seized it in its jaws and streaked through the
rent man's legs into the garden.

Three seconds later ex-RSM Denton's air rifle cracked,
and the despairing cry 'Missed the bastard!' revealed the
route the cat had taken.

Both the rent man and myself found ourselves in a brief
tangle in the doorway and I ran home to lunch. We had
fish and chips. I don't know what the Thomas's had be-

cause it was some time before I could bring myself to ask and by that time Kenny had forgotten.

Many years later, when he and I had gone our separate ways, my mother was standing at a bus stop reading the *Swansea Evening Post*'s first report on the part played by the town's territorial artillery regiment, to which I belonged, in the North African landings.

Somebody touched her sleeve. It was Kenny Thomas, and his eyes were bright with tears. 'He's gone to Africa without me after all,' he said and walked away.

3   Needle Match

One of the more pleasant side effects of being a member of our profession is the fact that one is invited to play in charity cricket matches with real live cricketers. To me this is always a thrill, especially when I have been asked to captain teams containing some of the most illustrious names in *Wisden*. There is no sweeter moment that life has to offer than when I toss the ball to Loader and say, 'Have a few overs, Peter,' or inform Colin Cowdrey that he'd better pad up because he's in next wicket down. Not that they take any notice, of course.

But of all the matches I have played, the one that sticks most in my memory is a game I played as a boy in Wales. It was a needle match between two street teams, Grenfell Park Road and St Leger Crescent and was played on a square patch of waste ground.

There was only one set of stumps and no bails, and the umpire was a girl called Muriel Evans. She was bigger than any of us, she knew more about the technique of the game and her father was the local police sergeant. Muriel was not just an umpire, she was a form of insurance against broken windows.

My team, St Leger Crescent, batted first, and between the fourteen of us – ours was a very long street – we managed to knock up the respectable total of a hundred and sixty-five runs, including thirty byes. Their wicket keeper wore glasses.

My own contribution was four runs off the back of my head, the fielders being too weak with laughter to stop the ball reaching the boundary. I retired hurt and went home, but returned fifteen minutes later bandaged like a Sikh and fortified by a glass of home-made pop and a Welsh cake.

By this time we were all out and the Grenfell Park Road lot were milling around on the pitch fighting with each other for possession of the bat. My team stood aloof until they had sorted out their batting order – after all, we had a councillor and last year's Carnival Queen living in our Crescent and we felt superior.

Grenfell Park Road could only boast one celebrity in the whole of its length, Mr Haywood who taught science in the Secondary School, and his son was the captain of their team. He stood out from the others by virtue of his tremendous height – he was nearly five feet eleven, and as narrow across the shoulders as a kipper is between the eyes. His batting was the one hope upon which his side gambled for victory, and he elected to go in number twelve. He was so confident of the prowesses of his opening eleven batsmen that after seeing the first over bowled he went off to the ice cream saloon in Fabian Street.

I was saving myself for Haywood, my demon bowling had been responsible for many a mother knocking on our front door to complain about her son's black eye or swollen nose, all the direct result of my notorious bumpers.

My father was always on to me to take up a gentler sport like Rugby, but I had strenuously resisted all his pleadings. However, after being set upon by Billy Evans's irate mother one Saturday afternoon, I decided to reduce the risk and bowl only to those boys who were motherless.

Into this category came Heavy-foot Haywood, his mother having died years ago, and he now lived with his father and his 'Auntie'. We called him Heavy-foot because he always wore large laced-up boots, and you could hear him coming a mile off. Although one day he came home from school in borrowed plimsolls and caught his 'Auntie' in a compromising situation with the rent man. This assured his pocket money for life, his 'Auntie' not really being his aunt, if you get what I mean.

Anyway, over the years we had lived in the same district a long-standing rivalry grew up between us. He was a powerful bat and I was the fastest bowler for at least a mile around. We had played against each other four times this particular summer and had won two each. Now this was the decider. Our respective reputations stood or fell on the outcome of this game and the whole of St Thomas parish waited with baited breath.

Roger Llewellyn, their opening bat, stayed there for ten minutes, in which time he scored four singles and three fours, when his father came to fetch him. It appears he had been tampering with the gas meter. Anyway, he dropped his bat and disappeared in the direction of Kilvey Hill.

Muriel Evans, plumping heavily on the side of justice declared him run out and amid much grumbling his place was taken by Tommy Roberts.

He knocked up a useful twenty-five before being caught in the slips by Clifford Harris, who was not actually in our team but happened to be passing at the time. As he lived in St Leger Crescent we claimed him as being one of us anyway, and Muriel Evans's finger pointed to the sky for the second time. The other side kicked up a tremendous row, but Muriel threatened to call her Dad and they subsided into an uneasy muttering.

By the time Heavy-foot came back from Cascarini's the tide of fortune was definitely turning in our favour. Nine of their men were out and the score was only forty-four. Even as he watched the next two wickets fell quickly. Tony Rees's mother took him off to carry her shopping bags home from town when he had seemed set for a good innings, and the next man in, Elwyn Brookes, trod on his wicket trying to hit the ball on the third bounce.

Heavy-foot was next man, and I took the ball lovingly in my hands. This was my chance to clinch the game; after Haywood they had no batsmen worthy of the name. When he was out, that boys, was it.

He seemed to be taking a bit of time to come to the wicket, and then when he did arrive we all gasped. The bat he was carrying was the strangest weapon we had ever seen. It had a long rubber covered handle and had about four inches sawn off the bottom. The blade was bound in tape until not a glimpse of the original wood showed through and around it were three wide metal bands. His team mates were jumping up and down with excitement on the boundary and we experienced the sudden chill of impending defeat.

My first ball went wide of his off stump and he thumped it contemptuously for four. I took a longer run for my next delivery and rubbed the ball vigorously on the seat of my pants attempting to resurrect a shine which had disappeared four months ago. He treated the second the same as he had the first ball, cracking it into Mrs Gorman's privet hedge for six.

So it went on, over after over, every ball I sent down at him he belted out of existence. It was impossible to get past his bat.

'Come on, Larwood,' he kept shouting, as I trudged wearily back to mark – an empty salmon tin.

My head throbbed under the bandage and my glasses became misted over with perspiration. Still, I would not give in, and even when he had passed our total I insisted on continuing.

'We've won,' said Haywood waving his bat in the air. 'You couldn't get me out, could you?'

'I'll bet you my new train set that I'll bowl you out in the next four balls,' I said nearly crying with rage and frustration.

'All right then.' Haywood smiled, and all his boys yelled their encouragement. My own team were already leaving for their houses, fed up with the whole business. Muriel Evans disowned us all, and snorted her way home.

Needless to say he was still there after four balls. Then I began to bet recklessly and my box camera, my brother's boxing gloves, my football boots, all went in successive attempts. One by one the spectators drifted away and though dusk fell his wicket remained upright.

By this time I had forfeited everything I owned, and most of what my brother owned and so reluctantly I had to concede defeat. We could not see each other and I was bowling under arm owing to the pain in my shoulder.

'I'll bring the stuff you've won up to your house to-morrow,' I said to Heavy-foot, before stumbling wearily off into the darkness.

'All right then.' He was gracious in his triumph at least.

As soon as I got in the house I collapsed. The clout on the head was worse than was thought at first and it was weeks before I was well enough to go out again.

I had been expecting Heavy-foot along to collect his winnings and I was nearly out of my mind with worry about what my brother would say, having gambled away his gear as well.

However, he never turned up and I discovered that his father had, at last, discovered Auntie's fondness for the rent man, and had removed himself and his son to a convenient distance.

I never saw him again, but strangely enough I always feel a slight twinge of apprehension when someone calls at the stage door to see me and says to the stage door-keeper, 'Just tell him it's a friend of his from Swansea.' It could quite conceivably be Heavy-foot Haywood come to collect his debt, and for the life of me I can't remember what I did with my train set.

4   That Christmas and Elsie

It was Christmas Day and I was fourteen and suffering from a severe attack of puberty.

'Silent Night . . .' I sang, head held slightly forward to catch the ray of winter sunlight coming through the stained-glass window above the altar. Elsie Thomas was in the front pew with her mother and I wanted to catch her eye. 'Aaa-meen,' I intoned loudly, trying to catch her ear as well.

The choirmaster glared at me in the mirror over the organ keyboard. My voice was breaking and the previous Sunday it had cracked in the seven-fold Amen.

'If I want yodelling, I'll ask for it,' he had said. 'This is Swansea, not the Swiss Alps.'

Now I blushed back at him in the mirror and knelt piously on my hassock, wearing my 'Mickey Rooney as Andy Hardy being told off by his father' expression.

Elsie Thomas tittered and nudged her mother. The rest of the choir were sitting back comfortably waiting for the sermon to start, hard-boiled sweets already bulging in cheeks. I dropped my head and pretended a prayer while the Vicar said 'In the name of the Father and of the Son and of the Holy Ghost. Amen.' I then rose gracefully and sat back in Arthur Williams's lap.

'Gerroff,' he bleated, loudly enough to earn me another glare from the mirror and a further titter from Elsie.

I resumed my own seat and fumbled sweatily for a pear drop in my cassock pocket. Things weren't going as I had planned. I did a mental dissolve into the Church Social the week before when Elsie Thomas had swept into my life.

She was a new arrival in our midst, her family only

34

recently coming down from one of the valleys north of the town. She was blonde and pretty and had the lads at the Social swarming around her in no time at all.

I kept aloof, though. Jessie Probert had caught hold of my jacket.

'You go and join that lot around Elsie Thomas, and I'll tell my Mam you wanted to play 'Doctors and Nurses' in the coal house last Saturday.' That stopped me. Jessie's mother used to carry her husband home under her arm from the pub on pay nights.

'I have no intention of going. Anyway I'm doing my impressions later on and I've got to go and rehearse.'

I walked away towards the unheeded plates of sandwiches and stuffed myself. I listened to the boastful chatter of the boys surrounding Elsie. Wait until I do my impressions, I thought.

The Vicar clapped his hands. 'Take your seats please, our concert is about to begin.'

There was a clattering of chairs and faces all turned towards the little stage. I took up my position behind the two draped blankets which acted as curtains.

'First we have Master Harry Secombe who is going to give us a comedy turn. Master Harry Secombe.' The Vicar waved a plump hand and the blankets jerked slowly back.

'Hello folks,' I said nervously, my lips cleaving to my gums, revealing my teeth in a macabre grin. Laughter immediately rang out. Tinkling laughter from Elsie Thomas. 'Ooh, there's funny.'

I went into my impression routine. Stainless Stephen, Sandy Powell, Lionel Barrymore could hardly be heard for Elsie's continuous laughter. The others joined in, not really knowing why, because after all I had done the same turn at Church Socials dozens of times. But Elsie's laughter was infectious. I was so elated by my reception that I even gave an impression of our milkman, which was a mistake as he was sitting in the third row.

Then I swaggered back down into the audience.

'There's funny you are,' said Elsie giggling.

'Hush!' said Jessie Probert, 'the Curate's tap-dancing.' She looked furious.

I turned to Elsie and did my 'Mickey Rooney meets Anne Rutherford for the first time' look.

'I'm Harry Secombe.'

She burst out laughing again. Someone hit me heavily behind the left ear.

'A bit of order for the Curate,' said our milkman, smirking.

Elsie was now stuffing a handkerchief in her mouth, and tears were running down her face. I could see Jessie's mother making her way stealthily towards us.

'I'll see you tomorrow night at the top of Morris Lane after choir practice. Half past seven.' She nodded, gurgling away into her hanky.

I reached the door of the hall just before Jessie's Mam did.

'What's this about you operating on our Jessie?' was all I heard before I shut the door.

All next day in school I was in a happy daze, although no one noticed. My attitude towards learning was one of perpetual bewilderment only paralleled by the despair of those who had the task of teaching me. I took three years to make a wire dish mop in metal-work class. When I took it home my mother thought it was a clothes brush.

As soon as I saw Elsie that night she started to laugh. I hadn't even spoken a word, but she was off. She didn't even notice I was wearing my father's grey trilby and my brother's off-white mac with only two buttons missing and a slightly torn pocket.

I walked alongside her in silence until she had settled down a bit.

'Will you be my girl friend?' I was wasting no time in asking her. That set her off again.

'Ooh dear, stop it,' she gasped, clutching a lamp post for support. 'I've got a stitch, take me home.'

We had only been together about five minutes, but there was nothing else to do. As we passed Jessie's house her mother was at the gate. Elsie was still laughing and holding herself.

'Oh yes,' said Mrs Probert, 'using laughing gas to operate now, are you, doctor?'

I pulled my hat further over my eyes and took the help-less Elsie to her front door.

'See you in Church on Christmas Day. I'm singing a solo in the Carol Service. You won't laugh then.' I left her and walked home determined to show her the more serious side of my nature. After all laughter is not the only thing in life.

'Amen.' I came back to the present quickly. The sermon was over and my big chance to impress Elsie was coming up fast . . . my solo. After this, and the pink sugar mouse I'd bought for her waiting in my overcoat in the vestry, she'd have the sort of adoring respect for me that Judy Garland had for Mickey Rooney in *Babes In Arms*.

The face in the mirror was glaring again. I gripped my carol book tightly and opened my mouth.

'Noel, Noel, Noel, No . . .' On the fourth 'Noel' my voice disintegrated. It splintered into a thousand fragments. With it went my boyhood and before me lay a wilderness of pimples, spots and slow-growing hairs to be crossed before I could call myself a man.

I stopped and turned to the choirmaster pointing at my throat.

From the front pew Elsie's smothered laughs came in

waves. Someone else took over the solo and all eyes went back to the books. Except Elsie's. Her mother was guiding her swiftly up the aisle towards the door, giving her little thumps on the back to try to stop her laughing.

That's it. Voice gone, girl gone. Then I thought of that pink sugar mouse in my overcoat pocket and my face began to stop burning. I wondered if Jessie was doing anything that night.

5 God and Dai

When I first became a choirboy at St Thomas's Church, Swansea, I imagined that God lived somewhere beyond Kilvey Hill and kept His eye constantly upon me with only an occasional glance at the rest of the world. My idea of Him then was of a large, forbidding, old gentleman with a fat, round face and silver hair, who looked remarkably like the Vicar. This equation of God with the Vicar changed with each clergyman assigned to our parish until He appeared in my mind like a succession of chalk drawings on a blackboard, none of which had been properly rubbed out. At one stage He had a large belly, three legs, two pairs of spectacles, hair in four different colours and a face that was so blurred as to be unrecognisable. Then, one day I saw Him portrayed in the Michelangelo painting of 'Creation', which was reproduced in Arthur Mee's *Children's Newspaper,* and with a sigh of relief I settled for that.

There came a period in my childhood which reinforced my belief that God had me in His sights all the time. I was stricken by a series of illnesses – scarlet fever, German measles, Welsh measles, chicken pox. One complaint followed another, each one seeming directly attributable to something naughty I had said or done. If I swore, some minutes later I would start to sneeze; a deliberate falsehood would result in a bout of bronchitis. It came to the point where I would swing the cat by the tail in the garden, come back in the house, stand in front of the mirror and watch the spots start forming.

This led eventually to a period of almost monastic be-

haviour on my part, until one day, provoked beyond measure
by my younger sister, I said 'bugger'. There was no sudden
flash of lightning and it was six weeks before I caught
yellow jaundice. He hadn't forgotten me, but His reflexes
were slowing down. One particularly strenuous bout of
'mothers and fathers' behind the cemetery with Gwyneth
Jones brought no sign of retribution from Him at all. Well,
not directly anyway – He sent her father instead.

During the war, especially when I was on active service
in North Africa and Italy, I must confess that He was on
my mind a lot. I felt that He was on our side, and was
dismayed to discover one day that the Germans also held
drum-head services. I started throwing in a bit of German
in my private supplications just for safety's sake, and because there were so many prayers being sent up at the same
time, especially during a battle, I was afraid that mine might
get lost in the general babble. Thus a typical prayer would
begin 'This is Lance-Bombardier Secombe, H.D., 924378.
Unser Vater which art in Himmel . . .'   It must have paid
off because I came out of the Army safe and sound except
for a tendency to drop to my knees whenever a car backfired.

No one who has been as lucky in life as I have been
can deny that He hasn't been good to me. I only hope,
remembering that delayed attack of yellow jaundice, that
it doesn't mean that He has just taken His eye off me for a
while. Retribution may be just around the corner. There
is one tiny factor in my favour, however – I have a brother
in His business.

6   The Scars of Summer

One swallow may not make a summer, but sometimes just one day can make a summer memorable. A day into which is compressed all the ingredients of my perfect summer – sunshine, good company, freedom from care and a touch of the unexpected to add excitement.

There was one such day just after the end of the North African campaign which makes the summer of 1943 a contender for greatness. Our unit had been withdrawn from the mopping-up operations and we were camped near the beach at Carthage. The relief of not having to fight anybody, at least for a while, was remarkably heady and I found myself on that first day with time on my hands, a sandy beach, plenty of sunshine, free fags and permission to stand up on the skyline.

So, stuffing my German phrase book into my kitbag, making sure to turn down the corner of the page containing the conjugation of the verb 'to surrender' – I was obsessed by the idea that if I were to find myself in a tight spot I might say 'I am about to surrender' rather than the more urgent 'I surrender', which could have meant the difference between life in a *Stalag* and a paragraph in the *Swansea Evening Post* obituary column – I headed towards the sea, wearing my drawers cellular short in lieu of a bathing costume.

As I approached the beach I was surprised to hear the sound of a military band. To my astonishment, there on the sands of Carthage stood a complete German Regimental Band in a roped-off enclosure guarded by military police and surrounded by various members of the British First

44

Army, most of whom were completely nude. The band stood in the blazing sunshine for more than an hour playing selections from operettas, tunes of the thirties, and even 'Tipperary' and 'Pack Up Your Troubles', all the time encouraged by cheers, applause and cries of 'Good old Jerry!'. There was no animosity on either side, and apart from some good-humoured attempts by some naked lads to conduct the band with improvised batons, the whole dream-like incident passed off peacefully.

The sensation of utter contentment as I lay back in the sand smoking free cigarettes, shorn of responsibility, secure in the knowledge of a job well done, and being serenaded by the end product of that task is something which has remained with me all my life. So much so that whenever I hear a military band I have an urge to strip off my trousers and lie down in my underpants to recapture that magic moment. If one day you read 'Ex-Goon hustled away in blanket from Horse Guards Parade during Trooping the Colour' you can rest assured that it won't be Spike Milligan – he's kinky about string quartets. But that's another story altogether.

I suppose it is the relief from responsibility which goes to make a Great Summer. There's not much enjoyment to be had from lying in a deckchair at the sea-side, wearing your knotted handkerchief, if you have to sit up sharply every five minutes or so to count the kids. Perhaps that is why some of my best summers were the ones of childhood when I had no responsibilities. However, I find I have difficulty in remembering those golden days of my youth. They lie scattered like amber beads over the floor of the disordered bed-sitting-room which is my mind. Some lie trapped in the fluff under my subconscious, whilst others wink tantalisingly from behind the libido. It seems as if nothing short of a frontal lobotomy will get this piece finished.

Then I remember an old trick which is usually successful in springing the lock of my memory bank – I look for scars on my person. My legs, in particular, are to me what the walls of the Olduvai Gorge were to Professor Leakey – on them are chronicled the history of my childhood. A crescent-shaped lump of scar tissue on my left knee records the time when I fell over in the school playground and cried so much that the headmistress gave me a biscuit with a butterfly made of icing on it. A number of associated marks show of subsequent falls in the hope of another biscuit, which never materialised. Here and there various indentations tell of the hazards of playing school soccer without my spectacles.

Then I rediscover a series of cicatrices on my right shin, and it all comes flooding back to me – the summer of the Bicycle! It must have been about 1935 when I was fourteen. All my life I had wanted a bike and after a determined campaign of sighing over Raleigh and BSA catalogues, and threatening to run away to sea – an idea which seemed to appeal to my father – parental resistance collapsed about June. I was handed a second-hand Hercules with some considerable misgivings and shakings of the head.

At last I was free to conquer fresh horizons, the whole world from Kilvey Hill to Skewen Oil works was mine. I pedalled furiously up and down the hills of our neighbourhood. I paid unexpected visits to remote members of the family, descending on them trouser-clipped and sweating, stopping only for a cup of tea and a few slabs of cake, and then off, to go swooping away down steep streets named after Crimean battles leaving behind bewildered third cousins on my mother's side who usually only saw me at funerals.

In a very short time I knew more about St Thomas, Swansea than the Borough Surveyor. Then, when the school holidays came that summer I was off exploring the coves and bays of the nearby Gower Peninsula with my towel and costume strapped to the cross-bar, and the addresses of distant relatives as a hedge against hunger. It was becoming increasingly difficult to get people to answer the door when I called – the screech of my brakes was a signal for whole families to lie on the floor until I had gone. My appetite has always been legendary in our family.

But I was content with the sense of freedom that glorious summer, drunk on the wind that filled my lungs; though a little sore in the crutch with the rubbing of the saddle. I didn't need company that summer, I had my bike. I have never been as fit as I was then, with calf muscles bulging and my face and arms tanned by constant exposure to wind and sun. I had taken on the identity of my bike – I was a twenty-two inch Hercules with glasses.

All great summers must turn into average autumns, and that year was no exception. I got over-confident in my cycling prowess, and one day, attempting to pedal backwards down St Leger Crescent, I misjudged the sharp turn past the church and finished up in the allotments, having somersaulted backwards over the railings. The bike was a write-off, my shin was badly cut, and to add the bizarre touch which was needed to finish off a truly memorable summer, the only witness to my misfortune was the parrot in its cage outside the McKenzies' back door. It laughed so loudly and so hysterically that even I was forced to join in as I lay bleeding amongst the cabbages.

So it appears that, in my experience anyway, the ideal great summer should contain a German military band, a second-hand bicycle, plenty of sunshine, a parrot, and, of course, a scar to remember it by.

7   To be Honest

Court Usher: Do you swear to tell the truth, the whole truth and nothing but the truth?

Seagoon: Yes.

Usher: You're going to be in a right mess then, mate.

This little extract from a Spike Milligan Goon Show script* seems to sum up rather succinctly the prevalent attitude towards honesty. We live in the age of the half truth, the slightly bent statistic and the party manifesto, which is a combination of the other two.

One can only write honestly about honesty where it applies to oneself and one's relations with others; so, on the somewhat overworked premise that the child is father of the man, let us look into some of my own youthful encounters with the truth. It's not a pretty sight, I warn you.

When I was a lad I was an avid reader of Arthur Mee's *Children's Newspaper* and *True Confessions*. The first was ordered for us by our parents and the second was read clandestinely when they were out. One was full of tales of honour and Empire and biographies of people like Philip Sydney and Edith Cavell, and the other told of dishonour and seduction, never explicit but hinted at by delicious dots. I must admit that I found the exploits of Mrs X of Trenton, New Jersey far more exciting than the tribulations of St Francis of Assisi, who must have spent too much time trying to get the bird lime off his habit to have naughty dishonest thoughts.

However, we were brought up in the belief that it was

* From *The Goon Show Scripts* published by Woburn Press.

better to tell the truth and face the consequences than to tell a lie. As a choirboy I remember sitting through a sermon on this theme, nodding sagely with my Young Woodley face on, my mind switching rapidly from thoughts of what was for lunch to agonised speculation on whether I should tell my mother about being caught playing doctors and nurses with Jessie Probert by her elder sister who now showed signs of wishing to be examined herself. At twelve years of age I was too young to cope with a full surgery, and was avoiding both girls, who, to my mother's surprise, had taken to calling at our house and asking if I could come out to play. I was a junior Dr Jekyll who was forced to hide. I was saved from a head-on confrontation with the truth by a fortuitous bout of yellow jaundice, during which I abandoned *True Confessions* and settled instead for a less heady diet of *Film Fun* and *The Magnet*. Just after my illness the Probert sisters discovered an embryonic gynaecologist living in the next street, and I was spared their attentions.

Featured in *The Magnet* were my favourite characters, Bob Cherry and Harry Wharton, two school boys of immaculate character and impeccable honesty, and upon whom I began to model myself. I became an insufferable prig at home, telling the truth about everyone and everything until even my father, the mildest of men, was forced to comment. 'If young George Washington doesn't stop his self-sacrificing I'll sacrifice him myself,' he said, waving the carving knife one Sunday lunchtime after I had pointed out that there was more meat on my plate than on my brother's – a most uncharacteristic gesture. Mind you, calling him Pater didn't help filial relations.

This phase came to an abrupt conclusion after an incident in school. I happened to be in a form which was noted for its exuberance, and its rough handling of the unwary teacher. One particular afternoon we decided to play a prank – a word not indigenous to a Swansea Secondary School, indeed until I read *The Magnet* I thought it was Chinese for a piece of wood. The victim was the maths master, a bibulous gentleman who would come back from a liquid lunch, set us some work to do and promptly fall asleep with his mortar board over his face and his feet on the desk. On this day we waited impatiently for him to go to sleep. When he had done so we blew sneezing powder around the room, dropped two stink bombs and as a pièce de resistance placed a beautifully made imitation of a pile of dog droppings on his open book. Awakened by the sneezing and the smell, he took the mortar board from his face and prepared for battle. However, the sight of the mess on his book unhinged him and he fled the classroom whooping like a Red Indian.

Vengeance was swift, and soon the Headmaster faced a flushed, frightened form. 'Come out the boys who did this,' he hissed, glasses glinting. In true Harry Wharton style I stood up and went forward to the front of the class. 'I dropped a stink bomb, sir,' I said.

'Of course,' said the Headmaster enigmatically. 'Anybody else?' I moved aside to make room for the others but nobody volunteered. Twice the head repeated his request, and still no one came forward. 'Am I to believe that there is only one honest boy in the form?' I held my head high, as the rest of the boys shuffled their feet and whistled tunelessly. 'All right,' said the beak. 'You're all on detention until further notice. You, Secombe, come with me.'

I left smugly, expecting a lecture and nothing more. When we got to his study the head turned on me in fury. 'You're not honest, you're damned stupid,' he said. 'Bend over.'

It was then that I realised that the truth does indeed hurt. I received on my behind what he thought the class should have had, and with each stroke of the cane I cursed

Harry Wharton and Bob Cherry and the whole editorial staff of *The Magnet*.

Afterwards I found it prudent to compromise by crossing my fingers either behind my back or in my pockets whenever I was forced to tell a lie. This led to complications later when I worked in an office where one of my duties was to make tea for the other employees. I provided the tea, sugar and milk and charged a penny a cup. There was one snag – the head of the department would insist on drinking only Typhoo tea which was expensive and cut down the profit margin. Eventually I hit on the idea of putting a cheaper blend into an empty Typhoo packet and spooning the tea from it into the pot whilst he watched.

The first time I tried it, I brought the teacup and saucer over to his desk on a little tray together with a packet of biscuits. He looked up from the huge ledger in which he was painstakingly writing in different inks all the month's output from the colliery. 'Are you sure that's Typhoo tea?' he asked. 'Yes,' I said. I don't know whether any reader has ever tried crossing his fingers whilst holding a full tea tray, but I can asure them that it is not possible.

The resultant shambles would have had me fired had I not been called up that afternoon for service with the Territorial Army. I must have been one of the few people, apart from Mr Krupp, who was glad when war broke out.

I still cross my fingers when I go backstage after a not particularly successful first night, and I know I am going to have to be dishonest in order to bolster sagging egos; or when a customs official says 'Anything to declare?' My own youthful struggle and eventual compromise with the truth is obviously compatible with most other people's. Which brings me to the inevitable conclusion that all world leaders and statesmen were young themselves once and must have carried into adult life some childhood superstitions.

When Chamberlain waved that piece of paper in the air after Munich, crying 'Peace in our time', were his fingers crossed? Why did Napoleon always have one hand inside his jacket? Watch the next party political broadcaster on television; if his hands drop out of sight when he's making a solemn promise to the electorate, don't believe him. One thought has just struck me – if you can see that his fingers are at rest, he might be crossing his toes instead. I feel there's no hope for any of us.

8   Fireworks in July

Whatever happened to the crispy bacon we used to have before the war? Where are the liquorice sticks of yesteryear? In a world given over to deep-frozen ducklings and polythene-wrapped parsnips I wonder how the little shops are surviving. A lot have been turned into self-service centres I know, but are there any left like the ones of my boyhood?

As a lad, I did a lot of shopping for my mother. I would swoop down St Leger Crescent in my brown plimsolls, heading for Websters the grocer's, whilst my elder brother, full of guile, would sit at home reading, pretending to time me by the cuckoo clock on the wall. Even in the grocer's I would keep up a jog trot, occasionally making little spurts across the sawdust floor as I waited for the assistant to attend to me. I would pant out the order, 'Half a pound of bacon and a pound of butter,' all the time bobbing up and down amongst the sacks of flour and sugar, hoping that this time I could beat my own record of six minutes and twenty-five seconds there and back.

Then it was off again along Port Tennant Road, past the Post Office where my father used to draw his war pension, past the off licenses, Griffith's fish and chip shop and the Home & Colonial, feet skipping the cracks in the pavement. If I land on six in succession I'll be going to Uncle Harry's at Llangyfelach for the week-end. One, two, three, four – missed. Never mind, I'm allowed three tries. Slow the rhythm down a bit at the bottom of St Leger Crescent, then head down for the long pull past St Thomas Church – choir practice tonight – and through the front gate, to fling myself down on the sofa. 'Just six minutes and forty seconds,' my brother would say, looking at the clock for the first time in ten minutes.

We lived on a council estate overlooking the docks in Swansea, and our neighbourhood was full of little shops. Some were just the front parlours of ordinary houses where widows served sweets from rows of glass jars on pianos and slabs of Bournville kept company on the mantelpieces with the pictures of stiffly posed khaki-clad departeds.

Down on Port Tennant Road near the docks, I remember one mysterious shop, the contents of its window unchanging through the seasons, the yellowing cotton wool and tinsel of Xmas forlorn in the spring sunshine, the dummy Easter eggs incongruous behind hoar-frosted panes. They sold gramophone needles, pen nibs, boot laces, Crayol cigarettes in paper packets of five, and fireworks in July. Its dinginess was heightened by the presence, a couple of doors away, of a bright bustling Italian ice cream shop, where we choir boys would meet after choir practice and discuss the vicar's idiosyncracies over doughnuts and cups of milk-frothed coffee. I left my first tip there. A penny under the saucer, which the dark-eyed Taffytina accepted with a smile that kept me awake at night for weeks.

In the same street was a barber's who once announced in his window 'Have your hair done in the style of your favourite film star'. My brother dared me to go in for a haircut while the offer was on. I sat meekly in the chair as he tucked the sheet around my neck. 'Well, sonny,' he said, snipping his scissors in the air, 'Who's your favourite film star?'

'Rin-tin-tin,' I said loudly, for my brother's benefit. He ran giggling out through the door. 'Oh yes?' said the barber grimly and proceeded to shave my skull so closely that I had to wear a cap in class.

Fish and chip shops were naturally in abundance in our

working class locality. Big gleaming fish fryers standing
against the wall, white scrubbed wooden counters, and
extra chips if you brought your own newspaper to wrap them
in. I remember the battered tin salt shakers and the vinegar
bottles which made a lovely juicy sound when you shook
them over the fourpenny cutlets and the twopenny tails.
A lot of people used to go to Mr Griffith's shop, not because
his fish and chips were that much better then anybody
else's, but because he was such a dab hand with the chip
chopper. He would have a bucket of peeled potatoes to his
left, and with an almost continuous movement he would
slip a spud into the chopper with one hand, simultaneously
bringing down the handle with the other, creating a steady
flow of chips into a bowl underneath, and not one of them
with a nail on it.

His was an individual artistry, and his shop worthy of
three stars in Egon Ronay's Guide any day. But the last
time I was down there the shop had gone the way of most
of its kind, forced out of business by the big boys. There
were of course 'big boys' in our district when I was a lad
– Co-ops and Home & Colonials for example; but my father
did not like my mother shopping there, although she did
now and then for convenience sake, without telling him.
All his life he worked in the wholesale grocery business
from clerk to commercial traveller, visiting the little shops
in the valleys using public transport and his own two
feet.

'You can't beat the little shopkeeper for personal attention and quality,' he used to say as he soaked his feet in a
bowl of Wheatsheaf Epsom Salts.

He was right of course, but as my mother found then,
it is more convenient these days to shop in the supermarkets
or chain stores and it is probably cheaper too.

It is a shame though, that my grandchildren may never
open a door with a bell over it, shout 'Shop', and wait for

a dim figure to emerge from a back room, shuffling on slippered feet to serve them with a ha'porth of dolly mixtures, or gob stoppers, or sherbet dabs, or pear drops, or fireworks in July.

9   Bright is Right

> 'Two men look out through the same bars,
> One sees the mud and one the stars.'

That quotation from Frederick Langbridge is a pretty fair description of an optimist. The cynic might interpret it as one prisoner standing on the head of another, the better to see out, but let us not concern ourselves with cynicism.

No, my friends, I am seeking to bring solace and comfort to one and all. There is talk in the air of a Depression – and what does that mean? It means we might have to do without things that our parents never even knew existed. Is that such a bad thing after all?

The dictionary definition of optimism is 'a disposition to take a bright, hopeful view of things'. Let us then look first at the days ahead. If we have to do without TV because of power cuts, why not revive the art of doing shadow graphs by the light of a candle. You know the sort of thing – 'the butterfly' done by waggling both hands linked at the thumbs, or 'the rabbit' which is effected by raising the first two fingers in a V and crooking the thumb over the other two leaving a little opening for the eye. This can also be called 'the horse' or 'the cat' or 'the dog', depending upon the age and credibility of the audience. If by some mischance one happens to sprain one's thumb in the process, endless amusement can be provided for the rest of the family as they all sit around and watch it throb.

This old world of ours has gone through many perilous

times and yet it has always managed to produce a bumper
crop of optimists. King Canute was one; so was William
Tell's son; my maths teacher was another; an angler fishing
from a railway bridge; my history teacher; any Liberal
voter; anyone dialling Directory Enquiries yet another. In
my experience, the greatest of them all was Johnny Price,
my old Army mate.

He was a stocky Welshman who stood five foot two
inches high and had a craggy head almost too large for his
body. Nature hadn't been too kind to Johnny, but he was
eternally cheerful, full of snatches of song and always
chasing the girls, and though he never caught any it never
seemed to impair his optimism.

I remember one particular instance when we were
stationed in Aldershot. The garrison town had suddenly
filled with Canadian soldiers who had money to burn and
consequently were always surrounded by all the available
crumpet. The rest of us had no chance at all. The NAAFI
girls were all spoken for and the WVS ladies were too
intimidating.

The only one who had not given up hope was Johnny
Price, and sure enough he came up with a scheme. He
burst into the Nissen hut one afternoon and threw a green
beret with a Canadian cap badge on to my bed. 'If you
can't lick 'em, join 'em,' he said. 'Stuff that up your tunic
when we go out and we're away, boyo.' He produced from
under his own jacket the bonnet of some Canadian Scottish
Regiment and put it on his head. It came down low over
his forehead, the tartan band covered his eyebrows and
only the great swooping curve of his nose prevented the
bonnet from slipping further down his face. 'Hello, buddy'
he said in his idea of a Canadian accent. I groaned as he
swaggered around the room, rubbing his hands delightedly.
'We'll go to Woolworth's sweet counter where all the best
birds are. Duw, we're bound to click tonight, mun.' I

tried the other beret on. That too was big, but my steel spectacles helped to keep it out of my eyes.

We duly presented ourselves at Woolworths where, fortunately, there were not too many people about. 'Leave the talking to me,' Johnny muttered out of the side of his mouth. 'I know the lingo, see. Got a cousin in Melbourne.' 'That's Australia,' I said. 'Never mind, they're all Colonials.' His optimism knew no bounds.

A pretty girl sauntered leisurely forward to serve us. Johnny raised himself on tiptoe so that his monstrous head came clear of the mound of slab toffee and hard-boiled sweets. 'Hello there,' he said, pretending to chew gum. 'We're from Canada my buddy and me. From the prairies we are.' 'Oh,' said the assistant. 'Yes, yes,' he said, warming to his theme. 'Ride the range you know.' I stood mutely at his side as he warbled a snatch of 'Home on the Range'. 'How about stepping out with me tonight? We could take in a movie.' He gave a huge wink.

The girl stared at him for a long time then she reached down under the counter and came up with an enormous stick of rock. She hit him firmly over the head with it. 'There's no bloody cowboys in Swansea,' she said in an accent as Welsh as his own.

Johnny was quite philosophical about it later in the ablutions as he bathed the lump on his head. 'Bloody good job I was wearing that hat,' he said. 'Could have fractured my skull.' Always looking on the bright side, you see.

Another thing to bear in mind in the uncertain days ahead is that one should never take the opinions of so-called experts as Gospel truth. We were once told that our boxer dog was untrainable. He came back from an intensive course at an expensive canine school apparently as daft as he was when he left us. According to his report he was expelled for being naughty. Yet, six weeks later in Cheam Village when I told him to 'sit' outside a shop, to my great surprise, he did. He sat there meekly until I came out. The fact that I was unable to find the key word to release him from that position is of no consequence. And the laughter I afforded the neighbours as I carried the hulking brute in my arms for the half-mile walk home was the EPNS lining in that particular little cloud.

We must all keep looking on the bright side. Let us make sure that every lift is provided with community song books, that horse shafts are ready to fit on to our cars and that our legs are lagged for the winter. As for me, I've just managed to get hold of a bulk supply of rose-coloured spectacles. If anyone would like to buy a pair at a bargain price, I can be contacted care of Johnny Price, The Corner Shop, West Samoa.

10   Idiot on Parade

S omeone said to me recently – on Remembrance Sunday of all days – 'Did you have a good war?'

I was appalled, secretly, although I made self-deprecating noises at the time. 'How can anyone apart from Mr Krupp have had a good war?' I thought.

Yet I must confess that I'm the first one to try to teach our four kids how to march in step whenever there's a military band on the box. I've given up trying to teach the wife – she was a toolsetter in the war anyway. There's a joke in there somewhere, I think.

At Regimental Reunions I'm there with the lads, stirring up old memories. ' 'Ere – d'you remember old Okehampton being caught behind the NAAFI in Aldershot with the ATS Sgt. Major, and saying he didn't mind jankers because he'd just realised his life's ambition?' And remembering that Okehampton's real name was Woodcock.

It is amazing what the mind can be persuaded to forget, especially when reminiscing ex-soldiers get together. Skirmishes become full-scale battles, retreats turn into strategic withdrawals, mole hills become mountains – and when they've finished talking about sex they get on to the war.

I can't honestly say that I loved the war. I was in it but not of it you might say, and yet even at this distance I remember parts of it with a startling clarity and a certain rueful affection. . . .

We were about to embark on the Invasion of Sicily and our regiment stood to attention on a sandy parade ground outside Sousse in Tunisia.

Montgomery drove his desert-camouflaged staff car into

the middle of our parade. 'Bweak wanks and gather wound,' he said, waving his fly whisk.

I was pushed along from behind, finishing up right against the car, and directly beneath the great man himself, who now began to address us.

'Take your hats off. I want to see what you look like.' I struggled to take off my beret, hot with the knowledge that beneath it lay four months' growth of wiry Welsh hair. It had gone reasonably unnoticed within the fairly lax discipline of a unit actively engaged in battle, but old hawk-eye above me was not going to miss it. To add to the general decrepit nature of my appearance, I was wearing a pair of steel spectacles which had been repaired at the bridge and at both sides with electrician's tape, with the result that the frames sat on my nose at an angle of forty-five degrees. To complete my Hammer Horror kit I was also wearing a piece of plaster over a mosquito bite on my chin. My hair, released from its bereted bondage, cascaded over my face and ears in a shower of sand.

Above me, Monty was telling us that we of the First Army were now joining the glorious Eighth Army and we had a tradition to keep up. Cautiously I raised my head and looked up at him, trying to look committed to the task ahead.

'We're going to hit the Hun for six,' he said, slapping his thigh with his fly whisk. I nodded fervently. The movement seemed to catch his eye and he looked down at me. What he saw seemed to strike him speechless and we stood looking at each other, locked in a moment of time, the two opposite ends of the scale face to face – a glittering Goliath and a dishevelled David, but both on the same side.

I cleared my throat, anxious to break the silence. 'We're with you, sir,' I said fatuously. He shook his head slightly, as if awakening from a *petit mal,* looked away and carried on with his pep talk. But the pep seemed to have gone out of him, and soon, with one last unbelieving glance in my direction he was driven away wearing the expression of a man with something on his mind. He must have been reminded of Wellington's remark when watching a march past of his men — 'I don't know what effect these men will have upon the enemy, but, by God, they terrify me.'

During my six and a half years in the Army, the only other celebrities I managed to get near to were Spike Milligan who, like myself at that time was playing walk-on parts in battles; General Alexander who was playing the lead in the Mediterranean Theatre of War, and Randolph Churchill, whom Sgt. Ferris and myself captured outside Medjaz-el-Bab. He happened to be facing the wrong way at the time, and his paratroop helmet did look Teutonic in the half-light, and besides, who could believe a German who claimed to be Winston Churchill's son?

There was the time when our twenty-five pounder guns clattered into a little town in southern Italy. We were the first Allied troops the inhabitants had seen and I sat astride my battered Matchless 350 cc motor-bike like a miniature, mechanised John Wayne. The townsfolk stood either side of the dusty main road waving hastily made Union Jacks and showering us with fruit and flowers from their balconies. The lads in the open trucks were up to their ears in grapes and figs, but I found it difficult to catch anything without letting go of the handlebars. I slowed to a halt, pretending to wave on the traffic. 'Frutta?' I enquired of a buxom signorina leaning from a first floor window. 'Si,' she said, and knocked me off my bike with a well-aimed pomegranate.

Ah, but life was not all like that. There was one little bit of glory which came my way, though perhaps not the way I expected.

After the fall of Tunis, a Victory Parade was held in which our Regiment took part, and having been dismissed as too scruffy for the march past, I climbed up one of the palm trees lining the route. It was quite near the saluting base, and as there were a couple of ciné cameras pointing my way, I tried to wriggle into a position where I could be seen. My movements disturbed a colony of ants living among the leaves and I was too occupied trying to stop them marching up my shorts to pay much attention to the marching down below, or to the newsreel cameras.

I wrote home to my parents in my weekly air mail letter that I might be seen on the screen if they looked for a palm tree near the saluting stand. After about three months solid cinema-going my mother finally saw me – well, not all of me, just my left leg. She wrote to say that she was sure it was mine because the stocking was around the ankle and that's how mine always was when I was a boy, and did I get the balaclava helmet and the talcum powder?

I never got round to seeing it myself and I have watched *All Our Yesterdays* on TV in anticipation ever since. I want to point to the screen and say to my kids – 'Look, that's my left leg in Tunis.' There's not much chance of that now though, they've got up to the post-war period. Pity. I had a good-looking left leg in those days.

11   The Broken Spectacles

I gave the starter of the Matchless motor bike another vicious kick, jerking my stainless steel Army spectacles off my nose to shatter on the petrol tank.

It was dark and the track was very muddy, and the red light of the ammunition lorry I was following disappeared with a final derisory wink around the bend.

I whimpered suddenly, the darkness of the Tunisian night around me intensified by my short sightedness.

'Oh Mam,' I said, wallowing in a trough of hiraeth.

Leaning the bike on its side in the mud, I began searching for my spectacles, feeling around helplessly until a star shell went off in the sky and I was able to see a glint of broken glass. The frame was intact, but one pebble was completely smashed and the other was cracked right across. My last pair too. I sniffed away a dew drop and carefully put the muddied ear pieces in position, holding the cracked lens gingerly. By shutting one eye, I could get a kaleidoscopic view of the vague skyline. At least I could see a bit, enough to get me back to BHQ where Sergeant Jeff Jones would soon be shaking his head in quiet disbelief at the fact that I had got myself lost again.

Only last week I had mistaken a map reference and taken a small convoy of four three-ton ammunition lorries on a guided tour of the Herman Goering Jaeger Division, and back into our own lines where we were fired on by the Northants, for whom the ammunition was intended anyway. Fortunately it was night time and no one was hurt.

I blamed the bike for most of my misfortune. MC13 it was called officially, and it looked it. Bombardier Obie

Williams had christened it during our invasion of a beach near Algiers. He had chosen to drive off the ramp of the landing craft on to the sand at a time when the boat went astern about ten feet, causing him to disappear into the Med. still astride the bike, and wearing full battle order. From then on, MC13 was shunned by the despatch riders and only used by the Command Post staff, who were sometimes pressed into service for simple escort duties. These past few weeks it had been my turn, and this was the last straw, this convoy. We were returning from delivering rations and ammo. to a forward gun position, and I had stalled so many times that the Sergeant in the leading truck behind me told me to get out of the bloody way and follow on behind.

Lifting up the bike, I cautiously mounted. Keeping my head stiff so that the cracked glass would stay in position, I kicked the starter. This time it roared into life, too loudly for my liking, as sound seemed to travel faster in the front line than anywhere else, and as nobody at that time knew exactly where the front line was, I was anxious to be off.

'Good job I'm wearing my Braille socks,' I thought joylessly, as I slowly put-putted my way through the mud.

An hour later I crashed into the back of the water truck.

'I'm home!' I shouted.

'Bloody lunatic,' muttered Gunner George Thomas, who was sleeping in the front of the truck. He'd never liked me because I could sing higher than he could.

The following morning I reported sick.

The MO had set up his surgery in an old barn, where he sat shivering, partly with cold, but mostly with a hangover from the Officers' Mess punch bowl. He was a martyr to drink, and he never asked you to cough first thing in the morning because he couldn't stand the noise.

I was the last man in, and he looked up at me with an effort.

I saluted smartly, and the remaining lens in my battered spectacle frame fell to the floor in pieces.

'What's the matter with you Secombe?'

'I've broken my glasses, sir,' I said, still standing to attention.

'I can see that, man, I saw it happen. I mean, where do you have the pain?'

'Nowhere, sir,' I replied, peering uncertainly at him.

'It's my glasses – they're broken, sir.'

'I've always known you were a damn fool boy, but pull yourself together.' He had once caught me doing an impression of him at a NAAFI soirée.

I began to explain what had happened the previous night, and that I was completely useless without my glasses, and as I was an observation post assistant, I would be unable to see any attacks about to be launched, or indeed identify friend or foe beyond a distance of six feet.

'German uniforms are a different colour, boy.' The MO was confused.

'Yes, but Americans wear helmets like Germans, and they are on our side.' The conversation was getting out of hand.

'Shut up!' He massaged his head with his hands and sat quietly for a minute. Then he shuddered and gave a little sigh.

'I'm not well today.'

I made a sympathetic noise and he fixed me with a yellow eyeball.

'All right – you'll have to go back to Soukh Ahras to get yourself fixed up with new glasses. There's an ambulance leaving from RHQ at eleven.' He paused and scribbled on a form. 'Take this with you and for God's sake keep out of my way when you get back.'

I saluted smartly, about turned, and walked into the wall.

'Get out!'

I stumbled out through the tarpaulin covering the entrance, and made for the billet. He stood, blurred, in the doorway.

'Germans wear jackboots,' he shouted in triumph.

The ambulance bumped its way over the rough track to the rail-head, where we were to entrain for Soukh Ahras, sixty miles down the line in Algeria. Inside, five of us sat quietly – I had been assigned the role of 'walking wounded' as there was no category for what ailed me. Across from me a Private of the Argylls sat with a bandaged face, next to him a despatch rider winced from a wound in his arm. By my side a Gunner coughed and spat noisily. He looked at me and winked, tapping his chest.

'Bronchitis, mate. Should keep me out of action for a week or two. Might even develop pneumonia with a bit of luck.'

I nodded, forcing myself to look ill. The ambulance hit a bump and the despatch rider groaned.

'Bleeding driver. It's all right for him, there's nothing wrong with him. Got a bit of shrapnel in the shoulder meself.' This came from a Bombardier from my own battery on the other side of me.

'Got a fag, chum?'

I fumbled in the breast pocket of my battle dress and brought out a packet of Players my mother had sent along with a balaclava helmet and a bar of soap. The fags tasted strongly of soap and the helmet was too small. I lost the soap.

'Thanks.' The Gunner with bronchitis leaned over and helped himself to the packet. 'Might 'elp the old chest along.'

'What's wrong with you, mate?' This was the Bombardier with the shrapnel again.

I waited, hoping for another bump. It did not come. I coughed.

'Chest?' asked bronchial Bill.

I shook my head.

'Shell shock?' The Argyll with the bandaged face was beginning to take an interest.

Again I shook my head, trying to get further back in the shadow of the stretcher above me.

'Malaria?' It was getting like a medical quiz game.

'You'll never guess.' I pretended to enjoy the questioning.

'Bleeding piles.' The despatch rider was not amused by the conversation.

Then when I was about to find something exotic wrong with myself, the Bombardier took a long look at me.

' 'Ere – you're Lance Bombardier Secombe, aren't yer? The one that does the turn in the NAAFI. I didn't know you without yer glasses.'

'I broke them,' I said, too quickly.

'Blimey, 'e's broken 'is glasses. Is that all that's wrong with 'im?' The bronchial Gunner's voice was tinged with admiration.

'Well, I've also got a nasty boil coming up on the back of my neck.' It was the best I could do.

I was saved from further embarrassment by our arrival at the rail-head. In no time I had concealed myself in a compartment with half a dozen assorted cases of severe eczema; dhobi's itch; and a sergeant who was only too glad to tell us what he had, and the good time he had had in getting it.

We arrived at Soukh Ahras about seven o'clock at night in the middle of an air-raid and heavy rumours that para-troops had landed in the vicinity.

A fussy Sergeant herded us into some semblance of order in the station waiting-room, where we shuffled forward to present our medical papers to a harassed RAMC Officer.

Without glasses I had no idea of where I was supposed to be, and was led eventually to a lorry which deposited about twenty of us at a school which had been turned into a hospital.

All the time, anti-aircraft guns were firing and lights were dimmed as low as possible. There was a general atmosphere of impending action, borne out by the new slit trenches being dug outside the school and the sandbags being filled by Arabs and soldiers alike.

We were again relieved of our medical documents and had our names ticked off on sheets, until I found myself propelled along a passage into a medical ward, where I was given a pair of pyjamas and my uniform was taken from me. By this time I was utterly worn out, having spent nearly four months in action, and confused by not being able to see what was going on.

I sank gratefully into bed, delighted by the feel of the mattress and the sensuous pleasure of linen sheets.

'This is the way to treat the troops,' I thought happily.

The rest of the night was spent in complete and utter oblivion, and so was most of the morning, although I did remember being awakened to drink something in a tall glass, and then falling fast asleep again.

The next thing I knew was a Medical Officer standing over me, a stethoscope hanging from his neck.

'Well, Brown, how are you feeling now?'

'What, sir?' I was still dozy.

'Fusilier Brown, sit up and answer the doctor. A full-bodied matron was at the MO's side – unfortunately it was a man.

'I'm not Brown, sir. I'm Lance Bombardier Secombe.'

The doctor looked again at a chart at the foot of the bed.

'Haven't you got dysentery then?'

'I've broken my glasses, sir.'

'Get out of that bloody bed, man – *NOW*!' The matron was furious.

Before I had fully recovered from the shock, I had been

stripped of my pyjamas, and my uniform, by now deloused and smelling of DDT was flung at me.

'Get dressed at once,' said an effeminate orderly. 'Ooh, they haven't half got it in for you.'

'It's not my fault.' I struggled into my trousers, attempting to conceal as much of myself as possible from the orderly's prying eyes. 'They must have got the names mixed up.'

'They certainly did, dear. Poor Fusilier Brown's been digging trenches all night, and then this morning he was fitted out with glasses. He must have thought it was a new cure for dysentery.'

Two hours later I had been issued with three new pairs of spectacles, given with a warning not to appear at the hospital again, and put on a ration truck back to the regiment.

I had a companion in the back of the wagon. Bronchial Bill.

'Didn't work, eh? The old chest bit – wouldn't stand for it would they?' I was a bit stroppy myself.

'Nah,' said the Gunner, spitting in disgust over the back. 'Gave me some tablets and a bottle of medicine and sent me back. I'm not sorry in a way though. I was up all night digging trenches and filling sandbags with some poor geezer what kept dashing off to the latrine all night. If that's how they treat the dysentery patients, they'd give me a hell of a life.'

I laughed so much that my glasses fell off. They didn't break though. Just as well really, I suppose.

12   A Bomb in the Bed

H urry up buddy,' said Johnny Price impatiently from outside the canvas.

'Can't find my blasted gaiters.' I banged my head for the umpteenth time against the iron framework of the three ton truck which had been our home all the way across North Africa and three quarters of Sicily. The perspiration streamed from me, clouding my glasses with moisture and making the search for my missing gaiters almost impossible.

'Come on, mun' came Price's voice, 'the other guys will find the place before us.'

'Good luck,' I snorted as I began buckling on the oil-stained webbing gaiters which had been hiding under a pile of jerricans and a camouflage net at the rear of the lorry.

Price's face appeared over the tail board shining with sweat and twitching with anxiety. 'There'll be none of that vino left for us, buddy.' He wiggled his false teeth jockeying for position on his gums. As he turned away, his profile reminded me of an Easter Island statue. Indeed, had Thor Heyerdahl stepped ashore one day at Aberavon and seen Johnny standing ankle-deep in the sand he might have had second thoughts about the Kon-Tiki expedition. Known in the unit as 'Craggy Chops', he had been a cinema projectionist in Civvie Street and had been so indoctrinated with American films that his native Welsh accent was overlaid with a nasal Yankee drawl. He also had the disturbing habit of adopting the mannerisms of his favourite actors whenever the situation he found himself in was applicable to the roles they usually played.

For instance, when we were in action he was Cagney or Gary Cooper, getting off with girls he was Cary Grant or perhaps Mickey Rooney in his 'Andy Hardy' period. He liked having me around at these times – getting off with girls, not in action as neither of us was very good at that – because I always recognised the bits of dialogue he had pinched, and I used to hum the appropriate background music to inspire him. We were a well-matched pair of idiots, I can tell you.

The first time I met him was in Aldershot. I was on duty in the Battery office when he arrived as a replacement signaller from the Depot. The Sgt. Clerk was out at the time, so I had to take his particulars, etc., and assign him to accommodation. As he gave his name, rank and number, he answered with a half cynical grin which revealed a gap between his top set and his gums wide enough to take a large size postal packet. At the same time his right eyebrow was raised quizzically in a strangely reminiscent way.

'Cary Grant,' I said suddenly.

'Goldarn it, buddy, you guessed!' he exclaimed, beaming broadly.

From then on it would have required an operation to remove him from my back.

And now here was Price, alias Douglas Fairbanks Jnr. in *Gunga Din,* eager to be off raiding the nearest village for vino and anything else we may be fortunate enough to find. And as proof of what was uppermost in his mind, he was sporting a red and blue dress cap, much crumpled from spending months at the bottom of his kit bag, and looking very incongruous with his battle-stained khaki drill tunic and the shorts which reached down almost to his shins. As we set off into the blazing sunshine we looked like Laurel and Hardy in *Beau Chumps,* only not quite so tall.

'Are you sure that the vino place was open?' I asked as we trudged dustily up the track towards the little village.

'Of course, boy. And there's a smashing looking doll in the house across the road. Didn't you see her waving to us as we came past? We've got at least two hours before the rest of the unit arrive, and by then, buddy, we'll be sitting pretty.' Price quickened his step as he talked, the dress cap jogging up and down on his plateau-shaped head.

I shook my head silently. The signals officer had gone back to report the unit, leaving us alone in the olive grove with the truck. Most of the fighting was over on the island and we had come forward on a reconnaissance to find a suitable spot to put our Battery of 25-pounder guns. There were no other troops in the area, and apart from a distant gunfire over towards Mount Etna, the whole area was strangely quiet. Even the village in front of us seemed deserted as we marched in ragged step towards it, the dust, white as flour, rising in clouds under our boots and getting in our eyes and mouths. Johnny spat disgustedly and took out his large khaki handkerchief – a Christmas present just arrived together with a balaclava helmet and mittens and an anxious note from his Auntie Lil in Swansea telling him to wrap up nice and warm. He fixed the handkerchief over his face, and immediately became Tyrone Power as Jesse James. 'We'll head 'em off at the pass, Jake,' he drawled. My reply was a short one. My shirt was sticking to my back and I was already regretting this illicit jaunt. If Lt. Joe Cattermole found us absent from the truck when he got back we would soon be Humphrey Bogart and James Cagney in *The Big House*.

Daunted, Price muttered behind his handkerchief and maintained an injured silence until we reached the little collection of houses huddled together on top of the hill. It was soon very obvious to us that the village had been bombed from the air. Glass littered the narrow main street, and a

dead mule lay on its back in the middle of it. I envied
Price his handkerchief as we manoeuvred our way around
the fly-covered corpse. Not a soul stirred anywhere though
we were aware of being watched. A few more yards took
us into a little square with a fountain in the middle of it
and standing by it, filling a can with water was a girl.

'That's her,' said Price, catching my arm excitedly.
'And that's the vino place. The door's open anyway.' He
pointed across the square to a low, whitewashed building
with only one pane of glass miraculously whole in all its
four crooked windows. A face appeared briefly around the
open door and as suddenly vanished again.

I turned my attention to the girl, who had now stopped
filling the can, and was regarding us with a mixture of
apprehension and relief in her dark liquid eyes. 'What a
cracker!' I gulped. She wore the customary rusty black
dress which all the women seem to wear in the country
areas of Sicily, but she filled it in a way which made me
catch my breath. There was no doubt about it, from the
tips of her bare toes to the top of her black curly head, she
was terrific.

She smiled uncertainly, as we stood appraising her.
Price said, 'Leave this to me, son – you're too young for
this one.' Then, clearing his throat, his eyebrow jerking
wildly, he revealed his dusty choppers in a horribly roguish
grin. 'Hello. Nice dayo.' He belonged to the school of
thought current amongst most British troops in Sicily
which maintained that good loud English with an 'o' added
on to the end of each operative word was a good substitute
for Italian. 'Us,' he said pointing his stubby finger first in
my chest and then in his own, 'Englisho. Not harmo you.
Where vino?'

The girl looked at both of us, seemingly reassured that
we were indeed harmless. *'Vieni,'* she said, her voice husky.
She crooked her finger, and beckoned us to go with her

across the street. The back view was as good as the front, and Price placed himself immediately behind her. 'I saw her first, mind,' he warned as we followed her undulating rear. 'Perhaps she's got a sister for you,' he added, not really caring whether she had or not.

The girl stopped outside a shabby two-storeyed tenement house on the other side of the village. For the first time we saw signs of life – a little boy, trouserless, his eyes big with wonder, came to the doorway only to be snatched away by an unseen hand as we drew near; a couple of chickens pecked tiredly in the dust outside the entrance of the building.

In the gloom of the entrance way, a small knot of silent shapes had gathered, indistinguishable against the harsh glare from the scarred white stucco wall. As we scuffed our way inside, the figures dissolved into the darkness of the interior of the building. We stood now in a central hallway with passages leading off it and as our eyes became accustomed to the sudden change from the sunlight, we could see in front of us a worn stairway which led up to the next floor. The girl walked to the foot of the stone stairs, turned, and with an anxious smile said again 'Vieni.'

Price, his teeth clattering a tarantella accompaniment to his actions, joined her side as she walked up towards the next floor. 'This is better than the films, boy,' he whispered hoarsely to me over his shoulder – an admission I had never thought to hear from him.

When we reached the head of the stairs, she turned left along a little passageway and stopped outside a door. Then, turning the knob with her right hand, she stood to one side and motioned us inside the room.

Price was in like a flash. He raced across the threshold and then skidded to a halt, his Army size nines raising sparks from the tiled floor. 'Good God,' he gasped, his face going a sickly white as he turned to me. 'Look,' he said. I peeped over his shoulder, amazed at this sudden change in him. Then I saw it and became transfixed. It was an ordinary peasant-type living room, with onions and pepperones hanging from a hook on the wall, a picture of the Virgin Mary with faded flowers in front of it, a crude dressing table with a battered alarm clock on it, and in the middle of the room a huge brass bedstead. From a hole in the ceiling a shaft of strong sunlight lit up the centrepiece of our little tableau – a large, unexploded, five hundred pound American Air Force bomb. It lay at an angle on the bed, its nose buried deep in the springs, and above the confusion of the bed clothes we could see the yellow fins bearing the legend USAAF 1943. We stood rooted for what seemed an eternity, the silence broken only by a loud ticking sound, of which I gradually became more aware.

The girl looked at us, the expression in her eyes urgent and appealing, *'Portare via,'* she said, pleading with her hands.

'She wants us to take it away, Johnny,' I stammered. He blinked, then suddenly, frantically, he pushed me aside. 'That ticking – it's alive, it's a time fuse, mun,' he yelled over his shoulder as he made for the stairs.

Caught up in his panic, I belted after him. The girl ran after us, pleading *'Portare via. Portare via.'*

'We come backo,' shouted Price from the security of the other side of the street. 'Get helpo.'

I stood uncertainly at his side, my mouth dry. 'Abbot and Costello meet Frankenstein,' I muttered.

'What, what?' said Johnny his eyes wild.

'Nothing,' I replied, watching the girl who had come as far as the entrance and now stood with her hands on her hips, her attitude one of anger and frustration. She was joined by some of the other occupants who, as she began to berate us in a harsh spitting Sicilian, nodded to each other in furtive agreement. What she was saying needed no translation. We were cowards, all Englishmen were cowards. Any one brave Italian soldier would have taken the bomb away by himself.

Blushing furiously under the storm of abuse we beat a hasty retreat back to the square. The vino shop door was still open, and by entering and banging on a table we managed to get the frightened, unshaven proprietor to understand that we wanted wine – 'Quickly, plenty of it, and we give cigaretto in exchange. Savvy?'

Price and I avoided each other's eyes as the big raffia covered bottle of rough country wine and two chipped tumblers were placed before us. I poured out two glassfuls, silently handing one to Johnny, who drained it without taking a breath. I followed suit, but choked as the raw liquid burned its way down my gullet, and began a furious bout of coughing, spilling some of the wine over my tunic, where it left stains uncomfortably similar to the colour of blood.

My friend Price passed across his grubby handkerchief, shuddering at the sight of the stains. We sat wordlessly, drinking glass after glass in quick succession, until the warmth of the sun, and the inner warmth of the wine began its process of restoring false pride. 'It was much too big for us to handle,' Price began. 'No point in getting ourselves blown up, buddy. After all,' he continued, the excuses coming easily in the grip of the grape, 'it's a specialist job, removing bombs – especially time bombs.'

'That's perfectly true,' I agreed, gladly eager to redeem myself. 'Let them think what they like – we have no obligation to remove it anyway. It's one of our own bombs isn't it?'

Price nodded, his fifth glass rocking slowly in his hand. 'Still, she was a corker, buddy. Prettier than any film star, that dame was. Imagine what would have happened if we *had* been able to take the bomb away.' His eyebrow reared into Cary Grant's favourite position. 'The village would be ours, pardner, and everything in it. We'd be heroes, boy.'

I let my imagination wander. The wine fumes wreathed delicious shapes in my head, and I reached drunkenly for the bottle. Price's hand hit my shoulder with a resounding smack. 'What fools we are!' he cried, jumping unsteadily to his feet. 'That ticking – that wasn't the bomb, mun, that was that old alarm clock on the dressing table. Didn't you see it when we went in?' Dully I remembered seeing a battered old clock.

'That's right,' I said.

'Well then,' Johnny shouted, 'that ruddy bomb's harmless – there's no time-fuse. It's a dud, boy. If it didn't go off when it fell through the roof, it'll never explode. All we have to do is push the bed out of the door, down the stairs – they're plenty wide enough – push it down the hill outside the house and we are heroes! The village will be ours and all that therein is.' He always got a bit Biblical when he was excited – it was the chapel in him.

'Come on, boy, we've still got another couple of hours before Cattermole gets back, let's live it up!'

He grabbed my arm, threw a crushed packet of cigarettes on the table, and pulled me out into the heat of the afternoon. We lurched unsteadily towards the girl's place, the sun already bludgeoning our wine-soaked senses. Price was still singing 'See the Conquering Hero's Come' in his strangled baritone, when we came abreast of the house.

Outside the occupants were still gathered, gesticulating and arguing, the girl in the middle of them. They fell silent as we approached and Price, bowing low before the girl, said in a travesty of her language, 'We, portaree via.' She looked at us incredulously, then flinging her arms round his neck, kissed him soundly on the cheek.

'*Bravo, Maria. Grazie tante soldati,*' applauded the now

excited peasants. Another girl, not quite as good looking
as Maria, seized me, and gave me a garlicky kiss. We were
in, lads! All we had to do now was to remove a harmless
bomb, all ready on wheels to take away.

Johnny started for the stairs, the grateful Maria clinging
to his arm. When he reached the top he turned round and,
like Raymond Massey in *Things to Come,* he motioned for
silence. 'Mustn't make it look too easy,' he said behind his
hand. 'We'll get 'em to move across the street until we've
got the bomb safely out. Safely!' He chuckled and winked
a big eye at me.

He made all the others leave the building by a piece of
pantomime worthy of Chaplin at his best and then, dis-
missing Maria and the other girl with sly taps on the pos-
terior, he called me along to the room where the bomb was.
The ticking seemed louder as we entered, and Price
pointed to the alarm clock. 'Fancy us being scared of an
old clock ticking,' he laughed, giving the bomb a playful
clout on the fin. 'You get the far end and I'll take the
front – the bed's on castors, and it'll move easily down the
stairs. Get cracking, buddy.'

I moved around into position as Price started a loud
reprise of 'See the Conquering Heroes Come'. Out of
curiosity I picked up the clock – then I sobered more
quickly than I have ever done. The clock was not going –
yet the ticking went on.

'Johnny,' I began numbly, 'there's something you . . .'

'Come on, come on,' he shouted, his mind full of anticipation, and pulling the bed towards him, he began the
perilous journey along the passage.

I could only hang on nervelessly, as the bed bumped its
way through the door. The sharp turn left jerked the bomb
sideways, and the ticking noise stopped. The sweat broke
out all over me, my glasses slipped down my nose, and I
moaned softly. Johnny now had his back to me using both

arms to pull the bed along behind him, and completely unaware of any danger was nasally intoning 'South of the Border'.

'Johnny, please,' I choked.

He turned his head, sideways. 'Let's get this bomb out of here,' he cracked. 'Bomb, "bum", get it? South of the border down Mexico way. Yippee!!!'

It was obviously useless to get the message across to him, and as I was trapped behind the bed, I had to play the drama to its bitter conclusion.

By the time we had begun the descent of the stairs, I was a limp, sweating, gibbering wreck. Every stair shifted the bomb one way or the other, and I was praying mightily that the springs would hold the weight until we got outside. Through the doorway the rest of the villagers could be seen assembled across the street, excitement running through them like electric currents.

After a thousand years, the bed arrived safely at the bottom of the stairs and Price turned around towards me for the first time since we began the job. 'That's it, boy,' he grinned, 'make it look good now they can see us. That expression on your face would get you an Oscar. Like Spencer Tracy in the death cell scene from . . .'

'For God's sake, Price,' I said brokenly 'get on with it. Let's get this thing outside.' ?

He turned, shrugging his shoulders good naturedly, and we pushed our terrible burden into the street and the sun. As soon as we were safely in the street, I pushed Price to one side and shouting like a lunatic told the crowd to scatter. Seeing my face, they went rapidly to a position behind the building. Then like one demented, I pushed the rickety bed, the castors now loose and springs creaking madly, to the steep road which led the way down from the village. Price with his arm around Maria was watching indulgently. 'That's it, boy – it's all yours,' he yelled.

With one last despairing effort, I shoved with all my remaining strength and sent the bed careering recklessly down the hill. 'Get down, you fools,' I sobbed as I stumbled back towards Price. I fell on my face pulling them down with me.

Just then, the bed lurched to one side, pitching on its side, and with a bang that rattled every building in the village, the bomb finally exploded.

A black cloud of smoke rolled lazily skywards and the one remaining pane of glass in the vino shop tinkled gaily as it hit the street. I lay still, drained of all emotion, my glasses buckled where I had pressed my face into the ground.

'Dear God,' said Price's hoarse voice in my ear, 'it was alive all the time.'

I nodded, tiredly. 'I was trying to tell you but you wouldn't damn well listen.'

'You knew?' Price couldn't believe it.

Before he could say any more the villagers were upon us. I was plucked from the floor by my newly found girl friend. Price was clasped in a weeping Maria's embrace and the rest hugged each other, laughing and crying in turn.

In a very short time a table was dragged into the street, bottles of wine appeared from hiding places and from the look in our girl friends' eyes, there was promise of more to come – much more!

We had just sat down at the table to enjoy the fruits of our labours when the sound of a motor was heard. I looked at Price. He looked back, his face comically sad. 'Cattermole,' we said in unison.

Our lieutenant burst on the scene with a roar of exhaust and a bellow of rage. 'Secombe, Price – you're under arrest,' he shouted, almost inarticulate. 'We're moving on in ten minutes and here you are swilling wine with the ruddy natives. Get in that jeep before I shoot the whole damned lot of you.'

The now silent villagers watched us climb, shamefacedly into the vehicle.

Maria and her friend waved their fingers in a pathetic gesture of farewell, tears already starting in their eyes.

Cattermole, still spluttering furiously, let in the clutch and the sudden spurt of dust from the wheels blotted out the so recently wildly happy scene.

Price spat dispiritedly. Then he looked at me, a new respectful look in his eyes. 'Did you really know all the time about the bomb being alive? Did you really?'

I nodded, beyond speech, then remembering the bomb again, I was sick over the side of the bouncing jeep.

13   The Expendables

The unit had established a temporary HQ in a reasonably roofed farmhouse north of Termoli and the battery commander was trying to catch up with some office work between barrages. He waved a piece of paper at the RSM who sat on an empty ammunition box opposite him.

'Div. HQ want us to send an NCO back to Tunis to join a party to pick up the kitbags we left behind there. We haven't got one to spare have we?'

'Lance Bombardier Secombe,' said the RSM promptly. 'He's getting to be a bit of a bloody nuisance.'

He was right, too, as I agreed with the battery clerk who relayed the above conversation to me as he handed me my orders. I was getting a bit jumpy and had taken to throwing myself into slit trenches at the slightest sound of a plane – ours or theirs. One of these trenches had contained the RSM. I had also wrecked his motor bike by running it into a three-ton truck while looking over my shoulder for signs of German infantry. We were in convoy on a road thirty miles south of the front line at the time.

The battery commander also had good reason to remember me. I had overturned a Bren Carrier in Scotland on manoeuvres and he had happened to be my only passenger. He distrusted my ability as a soldier from then on. 'You're a damned idiot,' he had said on the occasion as we lay upside down tangled in camouflage netting, our heads inches above the swift-flowing burn over which the Carrier had formed a temporary bridge. 'Yessir' I had replied, feeling that under the circumstances he was justified in saying so.

The rendezvous was at Divisional Headquarters, which was comfortably situated well away from trouble and which carried an atmosphere of unhurried calm compared with the frenzied clatter and banging of a twenty-five pounder artillery battery in action. I jumped from the truck, stood upright for the first time in weeks and took stock of my surroundings. The farm buildings were virtually untouched and because it had been static for a reasonably long time, the headquarters' staff had made itself very much at home. Painted signs were everywhere and pointed to such Aladdin's caves as 'NAAFI', 'Corporals' Mess' and 'Cook-house'.

'I'm going to like it here,' I thought, stretching luxuriously before picking up my kit.

'You there!' shouted an irate voice, and suddenly I was not so sure. A red-faced corporal advanced on me at a brisk walk, and within minutes I was presenting myself and my papers to a languid lieutenant who looked us both over briefly and waved me off to a tent near a pig sty. There I met three of my fellow companions for the journey south to Tunis. They were a curious looking bunch, and I wondered why we had all been chosen for the job.

One of them was a short, stocky corporal from the Buffs who had a flattened nose and an air of bewildered belligerence. He shook hands briefly, introduced himself as Corporal Frampton and ordered the other two occupants of the tent to get up off their ground sheets and meet me.

'Fusilier Black,' said the taller of the two reluctantly. He had bushy black hair, a long narrow face with a pendulous lower lip and a nervous tic in his right eyelid. This gave him the appearance of winking wisely and was a potential source of misunderstanding.

The other soldier was about my height with a small moustache and projecting teeth and looked like a rabbit.

D

He held out his hand and smiled tentatively. 'Gu-gu-gu Gunner Wuh-wuh . . .'.

Outside a motor bike backfired and with one accord the three of us threw ourselves on the floor. We stayed down for a few seconds then slowly raised our heads and looked into each others' eyes and knew why we were expendable.

'Wuh – Williams,' finished the rabbit-toothed one, 'Anti-Tank.'

'Secombe,' I said adjusting my steel spectacles, 'Anti-War.'

The following day we met the final member of the party. He was the Royal Signals Lieutenant who was to be in charge of us, but when we saw him, we knew from the smell of alcohol on his breath at 0900 hours, the stains on his battledress blouse and the marks on his epaulettes where his third pips had been, that we were going to have to look after each other.

Our orders were to get to Tunis by any available transport. A truck was going to be provided as far as Taranto, and from then on we had to take whatever ship was going. Headquarters was anxious to get rid of us and we had no time to savour its delights. Within twenty-four hours we were loaded aboard an open three-ton lorry with the lieutenant in the cab next to the driver. Corporal Frampton had tried to get in there first, but the officer summoned up enough sobriety to order him out again. We suffered from this for a time as the Corporal roared and shouted orders as we loaded our kit. He mistook Fusilier Black's twitch for insolence until I pointed out to him that the man couldn't help it. After a while he seemed to forget, and he slumped against the tailboard and went to sleep. We other three were too busy searching the sky for non-existent enemy fighters to follow his example.

'Lucky bleeders,' said the lorry driver as he unloaded us at the docks at Taranto. We gave him the age-old two-finger salute and picked up our rifles and webbing equipment.

'Take these documents and try and find the traffic Officer,' said the Lieutenant to Frampton. 'I'll go to the bar over there and see if I can use the phone.' He addressed this remark to Fusilier Black who winked. 'Don't be so damned cheeky,' said the officer with a show of indignation and crossed the street, squaring his shoulders as he did so.

The Corporal aimed a savage kick at a dog which was rummaging around his kit. 'That's the last we'll see of that bastard officer today.' He handed the papers to me. 'Don't see why I shouldn't get pissed as well,' he said. 'You take charge of this lot and report to me when you've sorted something out. I'll be over there to keep an eye on him.'

'Just a minute,' I said, overwhelmed with responsibility, 'What about all the kit?'

Frampton turned to the twitching fusilier. 'Come on, you bring the gear over. And Williams, you go with Secombe.'

It was hours later that the Gunner and I finally returned, having talked myself hoarse trying to find space on a boat to Tunis. Eventually I had to settle for a disabled infantry landing craft which was going as far as Catania in Sicily.

The news was received in total silence by the other three, who were seated at a table in the seedy bar. Frampton and Black had their heads down in the pools of cheap vino they had spilled, and only the Lieutenant was sitting upright. I gave him the news and handed him our sailing orders. He nodded sagely, without taking them from me, tapped his nose with his finger and fell off the chair to the cigarette-end-littered floor where he immediately fell asleep.

'If you can't lick 'em, join 'em,' I said to Gunner Williams, and seating ourselves at an adjoining table we ordered a bottle of Chianti.

The sea trip to Catania should have been uncomfortable

because we had to sleep on the deck, but it was a smooth passage, the weather was fine and the fresh sea air cleared away a lot of the wine mist from our heads. Frampton became almost human, and even Black smiled between tics. Williams and I had become firm friends during our exhausting day at the docks, and he allowed me now to finish his sentences for him.

The Lieutenant, of course, was found a berth in the ship's officers quarters, and we saw nothing of him until we berthed at Catania. There we had the same trouble getting transport for the next stage of the journey, and all Williams and I could muster was a lift as far as Malta in a listing Greek tramp steamer which was going to Valetta for repairs.

We turfed the others out of a waterfront café only just in time to save Black from getting knifed by a Sicilian fisherman who thought he was winking at his girl friend. Corporal Frampton, who had been doing worse things under the table to her and meeting no resistance, was reluctant to leave.

'I was doin' well there, Taff,' he complained over my shoulder as I carried him out.

The Lieutenant was delivered to the boat with some distaste by a smartly uniformed Military Police Officer. We'd had difficulty tracking him down until, as a last resort, we tried the transit officers' Mess where they found him asleep in the Gents.

From Catania to Malta was a nightmare voyage. We were confined to one of the holds where the angle of the deck was at a permanent forty-five degrees. Fortunately we had been given a box of 'compo' rations before we left, and we did not have to rely on the ship's galley for our meals. These ration boxes contained tins of bully beef and vegetable stew, soya bean sausages and bacon along with a tin of cigarettes, chocolate, hard tack biscuits, and, if you were lucky, a tin of golden syrupy sponge. There was also a tin which contained tea, sugar and powdered milk already mixed.

We had to use the galley's facilities to boil our cans after we had been severely chastised by the first mate for trying to light a fire in the hold. The food we had was, as I said, far better than that which the crew had to eat, and as a result the rats on the ship came down to join us. They even tried to dine on us. A nightmare journey indeed, further darkened by Corporal Frampton's increasingly erratic behaviour. He kept leading charges up Long Stop Hill in his sleep, sometimes cutting off the careful line of retreat I had been making in mine. Fusilier Black refused to take off his Mae West throughout the trip, and God knows what private hell the Lieutenant was going through in his cabin above us.

We were all relieved and delighted to get to Valetta. The bombing had stopped and life was returning to some kind of normality on the island. From the deck we looked expectantly at the odd cafés still open amidst the rubble. The Lieutenant joined us as we docked, bleary-eyed and scruffy.

'When do we go ashore, sir?' asked Frampton anxiously.

The officer focused slowly on his face as if seeing him for the first time. 'Yes,' he replied at length, choosing the word carefully.

'Gawd blimey.' The Corporal spat over the side in disgust.

Across the harbour HMS *Rodney* lay in all her glory, and lean grey warships and frigates floated arrogantly around us.

We were not permitted to go ashore by the Naval Officer who boarded the ship. He examined our papers and told us that accommodation on the island was extremely limited and that we would be told as soon as room had been found for us on a boat to Tunis. We greeted this news with groans and were only slightly mollified by his sending us some bottles of beer and a bottle of whisky for the Lieutenant. Back in the hold, the rats scurried towards us like old friends.

The next morning Williams and I were on deck carrying on a nearly one-sided conversation, when he stopped in mid-stutter and stared across the harbour at HMS *Rodney*. He pointed to an Aldis Lamp which had just started sending a message in morse.

'Th-th- they are sig-sig-signalling t-to us.'

I knew he was a signaller, and was far more eloquent in dots and dashes than he could ever be in speech. I had no idea of what was being sent, but he started to get excited and motioned that I should get the Lieutenant.

I ran down to his cabin and half dragged him on deck. He peered uncertainly at the battleship which was now repeating the message and spelled it out.

'TO SS PYRAMUS AM PREPARED TO TAKE ABOARD ARMY PARTY FOR TUNIS.'

He turned away and his eyes seemed to be clear. 'Do you realise Bombardier, that we are to be invited aboard one of His Majesty's battleships. We're going to finish our little trip in style.'

It was the longest statement he had ever made and it surprised Williams and myself by its careful clarity.

I thought he'd finally gone round the twist, but Williams nodded vigorously in confirmation.

'We'll have to smarten up,' he said. 'Get the men on deck as soon as you can, and looking ship-shape.' He gave a little laugh. 'Ship-shape,' he repeated.

Williams and I clambered down into the hold and aroused the other two who were as excited as they could be after six bottles of beer apiece. I took my other suit of battledress from my big pack and put a fresh shine on my scuffed boots. The others did the same – suddenly soldiers again, a spark of pride beginning to smoulder in our demilitarised breasts.

We stood in a happy group near the gangway waiting for further news. Behind us a voice said 'All right chaps, fall in.'

The Lieutenant was a changed man. He had put on his service dress, shaved off the stubble he had acquired on the trip from Catania and wore an air of authority we had never suspected he possessed.

'You heard the officer. Fall in there.' Corporal Frampton, smart and shining, was anxious to prove his own transformation.

'Now listen, lads,' said the Lieutenant, 'we've all had a pretty rough time on this little outing, and it's fairly obvious to all of us why we have been chosen for this kitbag operation . . .'

We looked away from each other and nodded.

'But today we have been offered a most signal honour.' He emphasised the word 'signal' and we all laughed. 'We are going to be the guests of the Royal Navy and it's up to us to show them that we khaki jobs are as good as they are. It's very rare for this kind of thing to happen and we as representatives of the Army must be on our best behaviour. Thank you.' He saluted.

It was not a very good speech, but I was so carried away that I asked for three cheers. Williams was still on the last Hooray when the ship's radio operator came out of his cabin with a message in his hand. He gave it to the Lieutenant who read it, stony-faced. When he had done so he handed it without a word to Frampton, turned away and went below.

We crowded round the Corporal and read the message over his shoulder. It was headed 'MESSAGE RELAYED BY HMS RODNEY FROM SS EXCELSIOR.' That was enough for me. Obviously what Williams and the Lieutenant had read was not from the battleship itself. As it turned out later, the wireless on the SS *Excelsior* was out of commission and also out of Aldis range of our ship. There was to be no glory road to Tunis, no white bread from the ship's bakery, no fresh vegetables and no free issue Navy grog.

The SS *Excelsior* turned out to be another tramp steamer and though the trip to Tunis was a little more comfortable than our epic voyage on the *Pyramus*, it was no picnic. We never saw the Lieutenant again and were told that he was put ashore in Bizerta with a bad case of DTs.

When we got to Tunis we found that the warehouse where all the kitbags had been stored had been broken into and the contents scattered. We became aware of this before we actually arrived at the door of the building when Corporal Frampton spotted one Arab going past wearing an officer's Sam Browne, and I saw a veiled lady with a jug of water balanced on her head and a pair of stout Army boots on her feet.

All I found of my own belongings was my Palgrave's *Golden Treasury,* which was some consolation at least.

It took us only two days to get the stuff loaded on a lorry and we were back in Italy for Christmas.

It was great to see the old faces again, and the disappointment about not having any kit left soon faded from the minds of the lads.

'Marvellous to be back with you fellers,' I said that night as we sat around the fire we had cautiously lit. Then a shell landed nearby and I wasn't so sure.

14 The Audition

I left Swansea on the afternoon train the day before the audition and stayed the night with my cousin in Romford. 'You'll be nice and fresh for your turn then,' my mother said.

Margaret and her friend Betty, who were both schoolteachers, fussed over me and made me eat a large breakfast of bacon and eggs. 'Must have a lining to your stomach, boy bach,' said Margaret who taught French with a Welsh accent.

'He's got a lining to his stomach – we all have.' Betty taught biology.

'You know what I mean – he needs something inside him before he faces that old Van Damm.'

The mention of the name of the man for whom I was going to audition that morning killed my appetite and I refused a third piece of toast.

I was due at the Windmill Theatre at 9.30 a.m. to perform my Army concert party act. The letter confirming my appointment in reply to my request for a chance to appear at the famous shop window for ex-Service comedians was in the inside pocket of my demob suit along with my Post Office Savings Book. I took it out and read it again, adding an egg stain to the other grease spots on the small type-written page. It had been my favourite reading matter at meal times since it arrived the previous week. The girls looked over my shoulder and read it with me for the fourth time.

'Nine thirty it says, there.' Betty looked at the clock on the mantelpiece as she spoke. 'It's only half past six now, and at the most it will only take three-quarters of an hour into the West End from here.'

'Ah – but I like to be punctual,' I said getting up from the table.

'He gets that from his father,' Margaret brushed the crumbs off my jacket. 'He's a commercial traveller.'

'*My* father's a postman, but he doesn't stand at your elbow waiting for you to finish writing your letter.'

The conversation was getting too obscure for me and, picking up my imitation leather suitcase containing my props, pyjamas and one spare clean shirt for my act, I bade them farewell and headed for the bus stop.

I arrived in Piccadilly about half past seven and found that I had the West End to myself. It was a lovely sunny August morning and I wandered around peering at the posters and glossy photographs outside the famous theatres and wondering what chance I had of ever seeing my name there.

At the side of the Windmill Theatre was a large board with a list of famous comedians who had performed there with the year of their débuts alongside. By the time I had finished reading it, the sight of all those famous names had dampened my enthusiasm.

I wondered whether I was making a mistake. In my suitcase the shaving mug rattled against the safety razor as I walked away down Archer Street and the sound seemed to confirm my sudden fear. How would the great Mr Van Damm react to someone doing an impression of the way different people shaved? It was not a very glamorous act to set alongside the beautiful nudes and fan dancers who posed prettily in the pictures outside the theatre.

I went into a café, ordered a cup of coffee and sat down to review the situation. Here I was in the West End about to storm the bastions of show business armed only with a shaving brush and a take-off of Nelson Eddy and Jeanette

MacDonald singing 'Sweetheart'. At least when Don Quixote tilted at a windmill he had a horse on which to make his getaway – all I had was a GWR timetable. I took it out and checked the next train back to Swansea. There was one at nine-thirty, and for one wild moment I thought of calling the whole business off and heading for home. If I did that, though, I would never have the nerve to try again. It was now or never. 'Nothing ventured, nothing gained' as my Auntie Doris had written in my autograph book. She had also written 'By hook or by crook I'll be first in this book,' but that didn't seem to apply to my present situation. Perhaps one day I would be writing in autograph books – without the need for a quotation. Just 'Sincerely, Harry Secombe' with maybe 'comedian' underneath in brackets for positive identification.

I made my decision to go through with the audition. 'The die is cast' I said to myself. Then I thought that could be a good omen. The Dai is cast – meaning the Welshman has passed the audition. I've got that sort of mind I'm afraid.

The stage door keeper carefully scrutinised the letter I presented to him and sent me down the stone steps under the stage. The place was packed with hopeful auditionees of all kinds – singers nervously vocalising scales, conjurers practising card tricks with sweaty hands, and one gentleman in full Chinese make-up struggling with an enormous cabinet.

I went over to a short tubby man who had a list in his hand and gave him my name. He checked it against the names on his piece of paper and nodded briskly. 'You're on after the Chinese geezer,' he said in a gravelly voice.

'May I borrow a small table?' I asked tentatively. 'It's for my act.'

He returned with a small green felt card table and again

told me who I followed. 'Be in the wings on time,' he said. 'They don't last long on there.'

Thoughtfully I began to prepare my props, first placing a sheet of newspaper on the table then putting on it the shaving brush, safety razor and folded towel. I filled my shaving mug at a tap in the toilet and began to lather up.

'You should have shaved before you came,' said the tubby man.

'This is my act,' I said in a small voice.

'Good Christ!' he said and walked away shaking his head.

An earnest young man in a blue striped suit came up to me and introduced himself. 'I'm Ronnie Bridges, the pianist. Have you any music you want played?'

I handed him a tattered song copy of 'Sweetheart'. 'I do it in two voices. The high one is Jeanette MacDonald and the low one is Nelson Eddy. When they're supposed to sing together I do a kind of yodel.'

'Yes, I see,' said the pianist slowly, taking in for the first time my shaving brush and the lather I was now vigorously applying to my face.

'This is the first part of the act,' I explained, splattering him with shaving soap on the 'p' of 'part'.

'What about play-on music? What tune would you like me to play on your entrance?'

' "I'm Just Wild About Harry" – because that's my name, Harry.'

'Very good. Very original. I think I can busk that.' He backed away smiling nervously.

'Thanks,' I said, applying more soap to the brush.

By this time I had cleared a corner for myself and some of the other hopefuls were eyeing me curiously, glad to have something to take their minds off the coming ordeal.

One man of about my age, wearing an American-type

college sweater and carrying a clarinet, picked up my razor. 'Army issue,' he said. 'Been demobbed long?'

'About three months. Thought I'd take a crack at the stage. No harm in trying.'

'Me too. This your act, is it?'

'That's right. Seems a bit potty I suppose, but "nothing ventured nothing gained" as my Auntie Doris says.' Some soap went in my eye and I winced.

'Anyway, good luck, mate.'

'You too, mate. When are you on – what's your name?'

'I'm on next but one. Norman Wisdom's the name.' He waved and headed for the steps leading up to the stage.

I finished my preparations about five minutes later and carried the table carefully into the wings to await my turn. On stage Norman Wisdom played a few notes on his clarinet and fell flat on his back laughing.

'Thank you,' called a sepulchral voice from the auditorium, and the young comic picked himself up and came off stage.

He grinned at me. 'Can't win 'em all,' he said and left to make a fortune.

The Chinese magician in full Mandarin robes and make-up wrestled his huge cabinet on stage. He put it in position and shuffled down front with his arms folded oriental fashion inside his sleeves.

'Velly good evening,' he began.

'There's no time for that,' said the voice from the stalls.

The Chinaman straightened up. 'No time for what, Mr Van Damm?' he said anxiously in a heavy Geordie accent.

'All that cabinet nonsense. Can you do something simple?'

'Well, there's the disappearing coin trick. Flustered, the magician took a coin from a pocket in his voluminous robe and started doing a sleight of hand routine with it.

'Sorry,' said the dispassionate voice. 'Next.'

'Sod it,' said the Mandarin despairingly.

In the wings I had lathered myself into a frenzy watching the fate of my fellow victims, and when the tubby man, who turned out to be the stage manager, tapped me on the shoulder I raced on to the stage with my table. My one thought was to get the business over as quickly as possible and return to the safe clerical job in Baldwin's Colliery Office in Swansea – if they would have me back, that was.

'Everybody has to shave, except of course women and small children – but nobody shaves in exactly the same way. Take, for example, a small boy shaving for the first time . . .'

I launched into the well-remembered routine at express speed, splashing the glass floor of the stage with soap and water, determined not to take up too much of Van Damm's time. At any moment, I expected the dreaded voice to interrupt and tell me to stop.

Before I knew where I was I had finished the shaving routine and was into the duet with myself. Ronnie Bridges gave me every possible assistance in spite of the fact that I was so hysterical that I over-rode every musical cue marked on the song copy. Once or twice I was vaguely aware of grunts from the stalls and I could only assume that the impresario was having a heart attack at my sheer effrontery.

I finished in a welter of flying soap suds from my soaked hair, as I threw my head back on the last note of 'Sweetheart'. I remained with my hands held high as if in surrender.

'Come and see me after the audition,' said the voice without a trace of expression.

I nodded dumbly and, picking up my table, slithered off stage.

In the wings a tall effeminate man stood facing me with his hands on his hips. 'You mucky thing,' he said. 'I've got to dance on that floor later on.'

'Sorry,' I said.

'I should think so,' he replied, flouncing off.

The stage manager grinned at me. 'You've upset him, and you might be working with him later on – he's in the resident show.'

'Do you think I've passed the audition then?' I was incredulous. I thought I had been told to stay behind so that I could be ticked off for wasting Van Damm's time.

'If he wants to see you after the audition that only means one thing. You're in.'

I began to tremble with delayed shock. What sort of money could I ask for? When would I be wanted? I assumed a Zombie-like stance. The stage manager moved me out of the way gently but firmly.

Ten minutes later in a clean shirt, but with soap still clinging to my hair and blocking my ears, I stood before Van Damm in his office.

'Very original turn,' said the distinguished-looking grey-haired man in the smart pin-striped suit. At his side Anne Mitelle, his personal assistant, smiled kindly at me. I stammered some self-deprecating remark.

'What money do you want?' he said looking into my eyes and not smiling.

'Ah, yes,' I floundered. I had no idea what to ask for. In the Army I had been getting three and sixpence a day for doing this same act, and I suddenly remembered an old pro telling me that if I asked a high enough figure I could always come down. What was the most astronomical figure I could think of? 'Twenty pounds a week.' The words came out in the same soprano register I used for Jeanette MacDonald.

'Right, done.' The impresario stood up and shook my hand. 'Miss Mitelle will draw up the contract. Good luck.'

The rest of the proceedings had a dream-like quality about them. I remember signing a contract which specified six shows a day for six days a week for six weeks starting on October 17th, 1946 – my sister's birthday.

I left the theatre with my suitcase and walked three feet above the ground to Gerrard Street Post Office, with a chorus of angelic voices singing in my head. At the counter I wrote out two identical telegrams – one to my mother and one to Myra, with whom I had an understanding. 'BEEN BOOKED FOR WINDMILL AT TWENTY POUNDS A WEEK LOVE HARRY' I wrote.

Proudly I passed the telegram forms under the grille to the lady behind the counter – the heavenly chorus reaching a crescendo in my head.

'That'll be ten and ninepence,' she said in a bored voice, not even looking up.

The music stopped and I came slowly down to earth. I handed over a pound note. 'I'm going to be at the Windmill,' I said by way of explanation as the girl counted out my change.

'I thought they only had nude women there,' she said.

'No they have comedians as well. All the top-line comics have started there . . .'

'Hurry up, mate.' An impatient hand thumped me on the shoulder and I picked up my change and left for Paddington Station.

15   A Night in a Cell

E ver tasted a mug of cocoa made on a gas ring in a police station? What is more, have you ever spent a night in a cell? Well I have. (Pause for excited whispers and shuffling of feet.)

It happened quite a few years ago when I was living in digs in North London. It was an old Victorian house with pillars and wrought iron outside, and on the inside cavernous brown varnished passages full of echoes and with a multitude of landings.

When I first established myself there, I took a first-floor bedroom with breakfast at thirty-five shillings a week, then as my fortunes dwindled I began to rise a floor at a time to less capacious and cheaper rooms. The extent of my success at the time can be judged by the fact that I was now on the top floor in a room which also served as a store for the house cleaning equipment.

It was the day after Boxing Day and the house was empty except for myself and the housekeeper, the other boarders having gone home until after the New Year. The reason I had stayed on was because I had a cabaret engagement that evening at an hotel in Pinner, for which I was to receive the astounding sum of ten pounds in cash.

The contract had stipulated evening dress, and not being in possession of one, I had hired a dinner suit from a theatrical dress agency. It was not a wonderful fit, and the lapels had a patina of fine grease which shone brightly in the spotlight as I stood in the centre of the floor of the hotel dining-room. The audience was very unappreciative and

viewed me with eyes jaundiced by Christmas and Boxing
Day excesses. Even the decorations hung limply from the
ceiling and my air of desperate gaiety had as much effect on
them as the paper hats they wore shamefacedly on their
aching heads.

I finished my act in a blaze of indifference and went
immediately to the manager for my money.

'Here's your cheque,' he begrudged.

'Can't I have cash?' I said, having only three shillings in
my pocket.

'I haven't got authority to cash cheques,' he said grandly
and handing it to me he walked into his office, shutting the
door.

The walk to the tube station was a long one, and a slight
drizzle did not help to raise my spirits. I could feel the
water beginning to seep through the thin soles of my hired
patent shoes, and by the time I reached the digs a full
hour later I was thoroughly fed up.

It was now half past one in the morning and as I stood
fumbling for my key on the doorstep even the hard bed
amongst the brooms seemed enticing. I searched every
pocket of the dinner suit but found nothing except the
cheque. There was only one thing to do, ring the bell. This
was a vain hope, I knew, because the housekeeper lived
at the back of the house and was as deaf as a post. I
thumbed the bell angrily, the sound echoing uselessly down
the dark passageway. Five minutes later, when the battery
began to fade, I stopped and began to eye the pillars
speculatively. Above the portico was a window which might
be open, if I could reach it.

I had just got to the top of the pillar when a light shone
in my face. A policeman's voice from below called 'Hello!
Hello! What are you doing up there then?'

I waved fatuously with one hand and slid down again.

'Trying to get in,' I said. 'I've lost my door key.'

'Blimey, it's Raffles!!' said the copper in a heavily jocular tone, seeing my dinner jacket under the raincoat.

'Can you prove you live here? Got any identification on you?'

Of course I hadn't, only a cheque which was made out to 'Cash' and did not have my name on it. After a few more questions for which I had no reasonable answers, such as what was the housekeeper's name – 'Muriel Something' was not enough – he decided we should go along to the station.

As we walked up the street, the stealthy pad of my rain-ruined shoes sounded sinister against the honest ring of the constable's boots. Already I began to feel guilty and my stammering explanations about being a comedian didn't seem true even to me. When we reached the station the policeman took me straight to the desk sergeant who had his back to us. He turned as the constable declared with an air of triumph, 'We've got a real comedian here, says he is anyway. Caught him trying to break into a house down the road.'

The sergeant gave me a hard look.

'What's your name?' he said. I told him and then still looking at me searchingly, 'Just a minute,' he said 'weren't you at the Metropolitan Theatre Edgware Road about a month ago in variety?'

'Yes,' I said hopefully.

'This is him, Jack,' he said delightedly to the police constable. 'Remember I told you about the feller doing a shaving act, with the lather all over the place, and then singing at the finish? Well – this is the bloke. Just a sec, I've still got the programme here somewhere.' And rummaging in his desk he produced it. 'Here you are – Harry Secombe, the crazy comedian.'

I breathed a big sigh of relief and launched into a couple of top 'Cs' to clinch the subject of identification.

Wincing slightly the sergeant got down to details with

the constable and myself and we sorted things out to our mutual satisfaction.

'You might as well stay here the night,' said the sergeant. 'Here's a couple of blankets – take this mug of cocoa and nip down to one of the cells.'

So it was that I spent the night comfortably warmed by Government-provided cocoa lying on a cell cot.

The following morning I bade my uniformed friends a fond farewell and arrived at my chambers in time to catch the housekeeper taking in the milk. She looked at my evening dress.

'Where have you been?' she said archly, hoping to hear of some romantic assignation.

'In jail,' I said.

She laughed disappointed. 'You theatricals are all the same,' she said, 'always joking.'

'By the way,' I said 'what *is* your last name?'

'Raffles,' she said, 'Muriel Raffles.'

16 Milligan's Overcoat

I think it was the overcoat that sparked the whole affair off. It was Milligan's overcoat, and as I was at that time much slimmer than my present shape would have you believe, we shared clothes. We also shared a bedsitting room, which has now become, in the recounting of various anecdotes from the past, a flat. But believe me it was a bedsitting room – and the only sitting room was on the bed.

The phone rang on the landing early one Monday morning and I was informed by my agent, who for more than six weeks had been unobtainable, that I was working at last. A comedian due to appear at the Opera House, Belfast had fallen ill, and as all the good comedians were at this time fully engaged in pantomimes, I was reluctantly chosen to take his place.

'You'll have to catch the plane at ten o'clock for Belfast,' said my agent breathlessly. The shock of anyone actually offering me work was almost too much for him. 'The ticket will be waiting for you at the Air Terminal where you will have to be in an hour's time. And for God's sake don't forget your evening dress trousers this time.'

I had once appeared at Finsbury Park Empire on an Easter Monday night first house wearing a dinner jacket and a pair of brown tweed trousers. I had sent the evening trousers to the cleaners on the previous Friday, and when I went to collect them Monday morning I found the place closed for the Bank Holiday. My appearance that night had given my agent a violent heart attack and ruined my chances of a summer season at Skegness.

'Of course I'll not forget them, Mr Hardman,' I said and put the phone down.

It was now nearly nine o'clock and I had to shave, pack, borrow money off a sleeping Milligan and catch the airport bus at the Terminal. I bounded up the stairs and shaved very quickly. I was still doing the act in which I mimed the way people shaved, and my hair and my pores contained a permanent supply of shaving soap. Once, waiting for a bus in a shower of rain, my hair acquired a halo of fine bubbles – a sight which was greeted with superstitious awe by the other members of the bus queue.

Milligan turned sleepily in his bed. 'Can I borrow your overcoat Spike?' I said quickly, knowing that he had a nearly new black crombie which fitted me nicely, and acutely aware that my own demob overcoat was gracing the back room of the second-hand clothes merchant around the corner. He grunted. It could have meant anything, but I chose to interpret it as 'yes'. Then, picking up a couple of quid from the mantelpiece, I said 'Pay you back next week – I'm off to Ireland.' His nose became alive over the sheet, nostrils twitching as they always did when he began to wake – but I was off down the stairs before he could collect himself.

On the bus from the Terminal I caught sight of myself sideways in the side window. The black spectacles and the black overcoat gave me a sort of mysterious look I thought, and I slipped easily into my secret agent mood. Eyeing the other passengers keenly, I stepped off the bus at London airport, already playing the part, handling my brief case with my band parts, pyjamas and toilet articles as if it contained state secrets.

I half smiled in a conspiratorial way at the uniformed official behind the ticket desk and padded stealthily into the passengers' lounge. Feeling thirsty I went to the bar, which was being patronised by some loud American tourists, and putting my brief case carefully on the floor I asked in clipped English for a drink. 'What?' said the lady behind the bar. I had obviously clipped my words too short, so in an unnaturally loud voice I repeated 'A dry martini.' The American nearest me turned at my shrill plea, and at the same time I moved to fish out some money. The impact of our meeting sent his gin and tonic cascading down his sharkskin suit. I stood aghast and then acting swiftly I whipped out a grubby handkerchief, and began mopping him down. 'Terribly sorry,' I said, rubbing bits of lemon into his suiting. He stood, saying nothing, looking down at his ruined lapels, and in my confusion the handkerchief dropped to the floor. I bent to pick it up and on straightening, hit his American jaw sharply under the chin with my solid Welsh skull. The blood flowed freely down his chin joining the alcohol on his lapel. He brushed aside to move away from the bar and fell over my briefcase. 'Goddam clown,' muttered the American.

My vision of secret agent was by now completely dissipated and I slunk into a chair away from the rest of the passengers. Then I saw him. He sat facing me, eyes expressionless behind thick lenses, a seemingly sardonic smile on his sharp, foreign face. Obviously a continental, probably German by the cut of his black leather coat. He watched me malevolently. Had I played my part too well? My insistence on keeping my briefcase in my lap on the bus and my over-exaggerated caution at the airport may have been too realistic. Could he be a counter-agent?

I looked down nervously at my crossed legs and was chagrined to see a big hole in my sock. The gents toilet was behind me and smiling desperately at the other fellow I nipped smartly inside and adjusted my sock so that the hole was not visible. By the time I had finished the flight had been called and I was the last to board the plane.

The only seat available was the one next to the German.

I sat down, clutching the briefcase, aware of his eyes on it and believing by this time that it really contained something valuable. 'Fasten your seat belts,' said the air hostess taking the case from me and putting it in the rack. As it was my first flight, I became terribly involved with the seat belt until my companion, still saying nothing, sorted out my confusion. 'Thanks,' I said awkwardly. He nodded, chilling me with a gold filled smile.

The rest of the journey was uneventful except for the fact that I was ill in a paper bag, and I was glad when we arrived safely at Knutts Corner. As we sorted our luggage from the rack I saw the German reading the label on my briefcase. He nodded, his spectacles gleaming when I snatched it from him. This is getting out of hand I thought when I found that his taxi was following mine all the way into the city. We pulled up outside the stage door of the Opera House, and he drew up behind. I entered the theatre hurriedly and ran straight to my dressing room. His footsteps hesitated in the corridor then went on. I breathed a big sigh of relief and began to unpack.

Later, standing in the wings I saw the German sitting on the stage playing a zither. He nodded cheerily to me. It was Anton Karas of *The Third Man* fame. I nodded back, then went to my dressing room and was sick in the sink.

17   In Praise of Corn

As one of the plumpest wood-pigeons in the broad acres of British corn, I feel well qualified to expand on the subject.

However, to make sure of the actual meaning of the word 'corn' I looked it up in Funk & Wagnall's dictionary. It can mean:

(1) The edible seeds of cereal plants,

(2) A horny thickening of the cuticle common on the feet,

or

(3) Anything trite or banal, especially jazz played in a sweet or sentimental style.

This conjured up the picture of a limping Humphrey Littleton blowing his horn whilst standing waist high in a field of wheat, and not exactly what I was after. Then I looked up 'corny' and found it means: 'rendered in a banal, bland or unsophisticated style so as to elicit sentimental feelings'.

That's it folks – that's what it's all about. Show business, I mean.

'I say, I say, I say, my mother-in-law has one foot in the grate.'

'Don't you mean in the grave?'

'No, in the *grate* – we're having her cremated.'

'Kindly leave the stage. Can't you see I'm trying to entertain these nice ladies and gentlemen ...'

'Let's have a big, warm welcome for one of the greatest stars in show business. Someone you all know and love, whose name is a household word – Dorothy Dustbin.'

'I would now like to sing for you songs I learned at my mother's knee and other low joints . . .'

'I dedicate my next number to all those less fortunate than myself. In particular Mrs Elsie Pragnell of 13 Rosewood Crescent, Bexhill-on-Sea, who is stone deaf . . .'

'Waiter there's a fly in my soup.'
'Yes sir, the chef used to be a tailor . . .'

'Waiter, there's a fly in my soup.'
'Don't worry, sir, the spider on the bread roll will get him . . .'

That's corn, all that lot, and so is Gilbert and Sullivan and Puccini for that matter. I speak in praise of it because it is comforting in a complex, constantly changing world to know that some things remain unchanged . . . that the gentleman in the immaculate tail suit will always get the custard pie in a Mack Sennett comedy . . . that after devaluation the pound in your pocket will still be the same . . . that Buttons will never marry Cinderella.

Ah, pantomime! The ripest corn of all. I was initiated into its mystic rites when I played Dame in *Puss in Boots*.

I turned up, with some trepidation, for the initial read-through with the rest of the cast in the foyer of the East End Theatre where we were going to perform. My only previous role in pantomime was Fairy Queen in an army production of *Red Riding Hood*, in which I made my entrance on a wire – thus providing me with the exit line of a life time: 'OK then Gran, this is where I retire – I should fly off, but no one's pulled my wire.'

After being introduced all round we sat down to read our parts. As my first entrance was on page thirty, I had time to take stock of my fellow performers, and noticed

E

that one rather elderly gentleman in a long, blue overcoat was crawling on his hands and knees over the floor. I bent down and offered to help him find what he was looking for.

'Piss off, I'm Puss,' he said, not unkindly.

When it came to my turn to read, I suddenly found places in the script marked 'Dame does business with basket', 'Dame and Baron do "Not Here" gag', 'Magic Fountain routine with Dame and Idle Jack'.

I was completely unversed in the traditional jokes of pantomime, only having seen one as a child, and that was so blue that my mother took us out at the interval, although my father stayed on to the end – an action which earned him a cold fish and chip supper.

'Excuse me,' I said to the producer, 'there are a few things here I don't quite understand. What's the business with the basket, for example?'

He gave a long-suffering sigh. 'Well, when you first make your entrance on the horse – that's Jack and Arthur here,' he indicated with his thumb two men dressed identically in tweed suits standing unnaturally close together, one behind the other, 'you carry a shopping basket with your knitting in it. You get off the horse as quickly as you can, because of Arthur's bad back, and you say to the audience,' – (here he adopted a cracked falsetto voice) – "I'm going to put my basket on this hook, and if anybody touches it I want you to say – PUT THAT DOWN." Then you get them to repeat that a couple of times. Right?'

I nodded, pretending I had understood.

'Let's get on to the Highgate Hill transformation scene then. Dawn, this is where you play your piano accordion solo. We'll have it hidden behind a tree, and you say, "Oh dearie me I do feel good, I've found an accordion in the wood."'

I never did get the shopping basket business right for the simple reason that I'm so short-sighted that I could never find the hook to hang it on.

It took me a long time to get the part right too. I didn't believe in myself as Dame, and on the first night neither did the kids in the audience.

'It's a man dressed up,' was the disillusioned cry when my wig fell off as I tripped over the hidden piano accordion on Highgate Hill.

My next disaster came during the ship scene, when I came tripping down the deck wearing what I imagined would get a yell of laughter – a Groucho Marx moustache and cigar. There was a stony silence from the audience and from the cast.

I was so demoralised that I gave the wrong cue which set off a sequence of unexpected events. The orchestra played the music for the end of the scene, bringing on the Fairy Ballet ten minutes earlier than intended, and taking up the ship's backcloth revealing an upright Puss with his head off drinking a glass of stout. He tried to cover up by going down on his hands and knees and pretending to lap it up from the glass, but nobody was fooled.

After the performance, the producer stood in the door of the dressing room I shared with the Horse, King Rat and Puss – we called it 'the Pet Shop' – and shook with rage. He waved an accusing finger at me.

'You're no Dame. You don't bloody believe in it. And neither do I, or the audience out there.'

He was led away. Jack and Arthur whinnied anxiously, and Puss uttered a sharp cry.

'I tried to arch my back then,' he said.

'He's right, you know,' said King Rat, a thin, nervous man with scorch marks on his tights where he had turned his back too soon on a thunder flash.

'I know it's corny and old-fashioned, but you've got to believe in it to get it across. You've got to be a Dame inside. When I'm in this get-up, I *am* a rat, see?' He unwrapped a cheese sandwich. 'For instance, when you were doing the "I'm not here" gag at rehearsals you were sending it up, mate. You mustn't do that – especially with kids. Try working for real tomorrow – that is, if you are working tomorrow.'

I was and I did, and though I was no sensation I managed to get the kids on my side. What I had done the previous night was to trample on tradition, and an audience will never forgive an artist for that.

I got to like pantomime, and the aroma of wet knickers and oranges, which is so much a part of a children's matinée, is still sweet to my nostrils.

Gradually I became a Dame inside, and by the end of the run I was engaged to the stage manager! It took my family and three psychiatrists to get me back to normal again.

Jack and Arthur were to be seen for some time pulling a brewer's dray in Clapham, and every night for years I put a saucer of milk out for Puss. As for King Rat, he became an agent.

But seriously though, folks, what I am trying to say is that to be old-fashioned or sentimental or corny is nothing to be ashamed of. Who amongst us has not worn a much-loved article of clothing long beyond the dictates of fashion, or shed a secret tear at some sweetly rendered tune, or bored an audience of friends with an oft-repeated joke? There you are then, and while we're on the subject – how about a quick chorus of 'Land of Hope and Glory'?

8 Summertime and the Living is Easy?

S ummer shows come in three different sizes – the small, seedy, end-of-the-pier show, the medium-sized, elegant, top hat and tails variety, and the big, brash, family-sized star vehicle, expensively costumed, spectacularly staged and occasionally disastrously box-officed.

In the first kind, the principal comedian is probably someone who has seen better days and can be found most afternoons in the nearest local to the pier, recounting his past experiences. So you'll know where to look for me in a few years' time. There is often a husband and wife who sing duets and act like cooing doves on stage. Off it, however, they become birds of a different feather. Mr Novello's lilacs which they have just gathered so harmoniously turn to hellebore the moment they get into the wings.

'Can't you sing in bleedin' tune?'

'You can talk, you were so off key even the pianist noticed it.'

Then they will go back on stage and bow sweetly to non-existent applause.

To complete the company, there will undoubtedly be a conjuror who doubles as compère and spends too much of his spare time stuffing silk handkerchiefs into cardboard cylinders and retrieving white doves from the roof of the theatre to pay much attention to the soubrette, who will be in her mid-thirties and constantly talk about her one television appearance in 1958. And that was on the Nine O'Clock News.

The chorus girls will be called Betty, Muriel, Shirley or Doris. The pianist will be a lady but will look like a man, or vice versa.

The second type of show is more genteel and a higher class of entertainment. The company plays Pavilions rather than Piers and travels its own wardrobe mistress, stage manager, musical director, but not, unfortunately, its own audience.

The content of the troupe will be similar to the first show, but there will be more of them. The principal comedian will be reasonably well-known – in concentric circles – and will have a stooge who will also act as dresser and drink his booze when his back is turned. The comedian's wife will not be in the show, but will sit out front to make sure that nobody else gets the laughs when her husband is on. This will cause trouble with the second comic early on in the season, and the company will then divide itself into two factions – those who are loyal and want to work with the star next season, and those who are disloyal and don't care whether they ever work with him again. The latter group will get smaller as the show reaches the end of its run, and will finish up consisting of the second comic.

The ladies of the chorus will be called Daphne, Fiona, Hermione or Susan-Jane. The musical director will wear a wig.

The star vehicle is brassy and big and designed for the largest theatres in the seaside resorts. It will have rehearsed two weeks in London and will be produced by a West End impresario. If it has a female singing star, the dressing room will have been completely redecorated, at her insistence, before she moves in, and when she does arrive she will complain about the smell of paint and develop a sore throat.

The costumes and scenery will be brand new, and the show is bound to have a grand spectacular scene where thousands of gallons of water are pumped twenty feet into the air. At the final dress rehearsal something will go wrong, and thousands of gallons of water will be pumped twenty feet into the stalls. The impresario will leave for London by ambulance.

The whole of the second half of the show will be taken up by the star, and it is a safe bet that before the end of the first week the microphone will have been changed at least twice; the first four rows of the stalls will be deafened by the amplification of the star's supporting group; and there will be protests (a) that she cannot be heard at the back of the theatre and (b) that she can *still* be heard at the back of the theatre.

The dancers, or show girls, will be called Midge, Jackie or Frankie, with a suspected Fred. The musical director will wear tight trousers.

It may seem that I am exaggerating, but I have experienced all three types of summer season and the audiences that go with them. There was the time when I was told by a flat-capped gentleman, as I left the stage door of a Blackpool theatre, 'You nearly had me laughing when you were on.' It was a compliment.

That is precisely the attitude to first nights I used to come up against when I was a second spot comedian. It was my job for years to go on after the opening and break down the resistance of the audience for eight minutes while the stage was prepared for the next scene.

I remember standing transfixed in the centre of the stage on a South Coast pier, like a small Welsh zeppelin trapped in a web of enemy searchlights.

'Hello there, folks. Welcome to the show. Are you all enjoying yourselves then?'

'Yes!' shouted the bass player who was drunk.

No one in the audience bothered to answer, because it consisted in the main of landladies with free seats, given to them in the hope that if they liked the show they would tell their boarders to come to see it. They sat unsmiling with arms folded and ears akimbo for the expected in-nuendo.

I have attempted to raise smiles from an audience which has had to battle its way in a force ten gale along the pier to get to the theatre. By the time they were seated the steam began to rise from their wet clothes, and I came out to face what appeared to be a low-lying swamp.

'I see we've got a good cloud in tonight,' I quipped. They sat in soggy silence.

Audiences vary tremendously in summer resorts, especi-ally towards the end of the week. Normally a show gets its best and biggest houses on a Saturday. Not so at the sea-side. Saturday is change-over day, when the old holiday-makers go and the new visitors arrive. Whey-faced and uncertain of their new surroundings they are more interested in settling down than going to the theatre. It is then, after the euphoria of a great Friday night second house recep-tion, that the blaze of indifference of a first house Satur-day re-awakens in the depths of one's soul the suspicion that there are more worthwhile things to do than trying to dredge laughs from reluctant throats that there is more to life than a belted aria.

Then comes Monday and a wonderful first house, and the journey back to the digs through the smell of fish and chips and candy floss, and the sound of raucous singing and breaking bottles of Tetley best bitter is a joyous one, be-cause if they were like this tonight they're going to be sen-sational tomorrow night. And of course they never are . . . but just wait until Wednesday.

19   Goon Away—Try Next Door

There was a young man from Cathay
On a slow boat to China one day
Was trapped near the tiller
By a sex-crazed gorilla
And China's a bloody long way

This piece of T. S. Eliotry was produced at a Goon Show rehearsal by the simple method of each person writing a line apiece. To many a puzzled listener no doubt the Goon Show appeared to have been written in the same way.

Actually, Spike Milligan would work all week writing the script, sometimes assisted by Larry Stephens or Eric Sykes, and Peter Sellers and I would only come into the picture on the Sunday afternoon before recording the show in the evening. Let us take a typical day. . . .

I roll up at the Camden Theatre in North London at about two-thirty, and my first thought is to wonder what conveyance Peter has arrived in. He was always changing his cars. One Sunday it might be a Goggomobile, and the next an Austin Princess. I believe at one time he was negotiating to buy a steam-roller.

As I enter the stage door, conveniently next door to a pub, I sing a burst of *Return to Sorrento.* There come cries of 'It's Singo, the approaching tenor, folks' from Sellers, who is playing the bongos in a prone position, accompanying Milligan's frenzied piano playing. 'Ah! The well-known danger to shipping has arrived. Ned of Wales is here.' Milligan announces my arrival with a NAAFI pianist's version of *We'll Keep A Welcome.* 'They'll never take you back, Ned.'

I reply with a raspberry. 'He's ad libbing again,' says Spike. 'Nurse, the screens – at once.' Bloodnock Sellers is now using the bongo drums as a pair of binoculars.

There follows a rapid exchange of Army jokes and the latest gags, mostly of scatalogical nature.

'All right lads, that's enough.' John Browell appears in the auditorium. He is the producer and it shows in the worry lines on his forehead. 'Let's have a look at the script.' With cries of 'Cobblers' and 'Ying ton Iddle I Po' we retire to a back room in the theatre where we are given scripts.

This was always the best time for us. It made everything worth while – the frustration of tackling audiences in variety theatres where we were still finding it difficult to establish ourselves with a public accustomed to a less frenetic kind of comedy, or having to deal with managements who were completely against what we were trying to do – understandably perhaps, because we were not sure ourselves. Ours was a kind of anarchy in comedy. We were against the established form of presentation. At the time when we began the Goon Show in 1951, the profession was full of stand-up comics who came on and told a string of jokes and finished either with a song or a dance.

Our approach was different. We had spent the war years with lads of our own age in the Services and we had fresh ideas. We were all first generation show business – apart from Peter, whose family was connected with the Theatre. Perhaps I had better go back to when it all began.

Spike was born in Burma, and was the son of a Warrant Officer in the Indian Army.

When I first met him, he was Lance-Sergeant Milligan, Terence A., and one of the crew of a large 7.2 gun howitzer which had been installed in a gun-pit insecurely dug in the hard rock of a Tunisian plateau. His howitzer was being fired by a lanyard — a rope attached to the firing lever which was used when the gun crew were not quite sure of what might happen. It was night time, and the crew left the gun while the 'No. 1' of the gun, a sergeant, pulled the lanyard. The crew turned their backs to the gun as it fired, and when they turned round, it had disappeared.

At that time I was in an Artillery Regiment deployed near by, and I was sitting in a small wireless truck at the foot of a sizeable cliff. Suddenly there was a terrible noise as some monstrous object fell from the sky quite close to us. I immediately began looking in my German dictionary for suitable phrases for surrendering. If they were throwing things that big at us there was no alternative.

There was considerable confusion, and in the middle of it all the flap of the truck was pushed open and a young, helmeted idiot asked 'Anybody see a gun?' It was Milligan, and our paths were destined to cross many times.

I have fond memories of Spike dressed as a gypsy with black-dyed hessian trousers, brown plimsolls and a red bandanna tied low on his brow, singing in all sincerity 'Down in the forest, playing his old guitar, lives an old dream man. . . .' This was in Italy after the war, when we were together in an Army show. In addition to being a comedian I also had to be a ballet dancer and ballad singer. I used to do an act which portrayed how different people shaved, later to get me into the Windmill Theatre, and later still to get me removed from the Grand Theatre, Bolton, where the owner told me as he paid me off on the Monday night, 'You'll not shave in my bloody time.'

When I was demobbed in 1946 I started at the Windmill Theatre, where I had the good fortune to meet Mike Bentine. He was half of an act called Sherwood and Forest, and played the drums while Tony Sherwood played piano. I first saw him when he and his partner did the dress rehearsal for the show which followed the one I was in. From the beginning we found we had the same sense of the ridiculous. We used to sit in the Lyons Corner House in Coventry Street and spend most of the night over a cup of coffee and beans on toast, sometimes pretending we were Russian. The game was up when we picked on a Hungarian waiter who spoke Russian.

When Spike eventually left the Army I introduced him to Mike Bentine at Allen's Club — a haven for Windmill performers. Here you could eat now and pay later, and sit and pour out your ambitions into the ears of other young comics like Jimmy Edwards, Frank Muir, Alfred Marks and Bill Kerr, who were simultaneously pouring out their ambitions. It's a wonder anybody heard anything. It was an exciting period when we were all keen to get on, but the rivalry was friendly and the comradeship of the Services was still warm.

Later at a broadcast for Pat Dixon, a professional-looking man who had an ear for unusual comedy and was always on the look out for young talent, I was introduced to Peter Sellers. Peter had recently got himself a broadcast by the simple expedient of ringing Pat Dixon and using the voice of another radio producer, telling him he was sending this new comic Peter Sellers along to see him. Minutes later he turned up at Dixon's office and was booked on the spot.

I was very impressed by Peter, by his friendliness and the uncanny way in which he became the person he was impersonating. Later, standing next to him on the Goon Show, I could never get over the way he would shrink himself for Bluebottle and then seconds later, puff himself out for Bloodnock. It was almost frightening to see it happen. Yet when he was called upon to do his own natural voice, he was always worried. 'I can't, lads,' he'd say. 'I don't know what I sound like.'

How the Goon Shows eventually got going is somewhat vague at this distance. By that time Spike and I were sharing a flat in Notting Hill Gate with two other fellow ex-Servicemen, Norman Vaughan and Johnny Mulgrew. Johnny played the bass in a comedy-musical act called Hall, Norman and Ladd, in which Spike was the guitarist. We all clubbed together to pay the rent and the hire of the radio set – although one day Norman Vaughan arrived back from a week's variety just in time to stop the hire firm from removing it. We had, however, taken the precaution of removing the valves.

This particular period returns today almost as in a kaleidoscope. I remember cooking spaghetti on a gas ring with the steam loosening the wallpaper; running outside and around the block wearing only a vest and underpants on a pouring wet November night, and nobody taking any notice; the hysteria which we generated among ourselves at our own jokes; Spike doing his impression of the last turkey in the shop; sitting with Spike and Norman in a café at Golders Green, and buttoning my war surplus duffel coat over my head for a gag, then five minutes later finding myself alone at the table facing an unamused waitress and the bill for the meal; going with Spike and Peter to watch Charlie Chaplin in *City Lights* and the three of us leaving the cinema in tears; drinking free brandy in Jimmy Grafton's pub in Victoria Street.

During this chaotic time, the Goon Show was written by Spike and Larry Stephens, and Pat Dixon persuaded the BBC to do a pilot show. It was called *Falling Leaves* and featured 'those crazy people, the Goons'.

I had to drive down from Blackpool, where I was in a Summer Show, to London for the recording on a Sunday. It meant driving through the night to be there in time for rehearsals. From then on I was known as 'He drives through the night'.

Pat Dixon produced the show, which even when listened to today is almost incoherent. To give the BBC due credit, they decided to take a chance on it, and so in 1951, with Dennis Main Wilson producing, it all began.

Meanwhile, back at the Camden Theatre. . . . We have finished rolling about at the script, and John Browell is wondering how he is going to control us. Wallace Greenslade is with us now, having finished his news reading for the day. He comes in beaming and ruddy-complexioned, with the lingering scent of an after-lunch Worthington on his breath.

'Sing us the news, Wal.' Spike has decided to stand on his head. Wally replies with a good natured Naval phrase. 'Hello, Sailor,' lisps Peter, looking up archly from under the piano, where he has retired for a short kip.

Spike now leaves for a chat with the effects boys. He is particularly anxious to get the effect of someone being hit in the face with a sockful of custard. They try several effects but Milligan is a perfectionist, he knows what he wants. He goes up to the canteen in the top of the theatre. 'Make me an egg custard, love,' he asks the very nice Scottish lady who runs the place. 'Of course, dear,' she says. Half an hour later he returns and asks for his custard. It is given to him by the Scottish lady who has prepared it especially, using the then rare shell eggs.

'Thanks, love,' he says, and removes his sock. Before her astonished gaze he promptly pours the egg custard into it.

Back downstairs again he arranges to have a mike set up. He bashes the sockful of custard against a piece of hardboard. 'Let's hear that back.' They play the sound effect back to him. 'Doesn't sound like a sockful of custard,' he says. 'We'll have to try something else.'

The musicians arrive, preceded by Wally Stott who looks too frail to pick up his baton. Ray Ellington enters with

Max Geldray. 'Good job you've got a long nose, Max,' says Milligan. 'It keeps the rain off your tie.'

'Ploogie,' replies Max morosely.

'Hello dere, Gladys.' Ray Ellington is using his Southern Negro voice today. The son of an American Negro and a Russian Jewess, Ray is having difficulty reaching a decision about whether to have his son barmitzva'd or baptized in the Anglican Church. 'Have a word with my brother,' I say. 'He's in that business.' It's my most useful verbal contribution of the day. Ray agrees to talk to the Reverend Fred Secombe.

We do a run-through with effects and orchestra. We have a little difficulty with the effects again. 'It's the Wembley Cup Final.'

'OK Spike, we'll sort it out later.' John Browell's soothing voice comes over the speaker from the control-room. Spike snorts.

The run-through over, Spike sits in with Ray and some of the band boys. Spike plays his trumpet, eyes closed and cheeks puffed out like those of a cherubim representing a trade wind on a sixteenth-century map. Peter has taken over the drums and is giving a creditable performance. I stand tapping my feet, wishing secretly that I had taken those piano lessons I was offered as a child: then I remember that we had no piano at home anyway. I go to the side away from the noise and sing a snatch of La Bohème. I feel a bit better, and stroll back on stage.

The queue has started forming outside and we head for the pub next door. Inside are the orchestra, friends of ours and Goon addicts, all of them would-be Bluebottles and Eccles and Neddies. 'Hello, my Capitain,' says one to Peter. He smiles politely, trying not to wince. Spike is complaining about his sock, still wet from the custard. We order drinks – brandies. I have a double. 'He'll be the first one to go, Mate,' says Spike to Peter. 'I don't want to be there when it happens; he'd rupture the lot of us trying to move him.' I blow a raspberry. 'Very nice, dear,' says the barmaid. 'Now do it with your face,' says a Goon fan with a delicate sense of humour!

'All back, lads.' John Browell herds us back into the theatre. We take a bottle of brandy and a pint of milk for the musical interludes, when we nip backstage. It also explains why sometimes the last part of the Show is the most frenetic.

The audience is already in and we start the warm-up. I sing *Falling in Love With Love*, accompanied by Wally Stott and the orchestra, and behind me Spike and Peter do outrageous things including trouser-dropping. I sing on, hoping Spike has not forgotten his underpants.

Wally Greenslade steps forward and asks for silence. The green light goes on. 'This is the BBC Home Service. Tiddly pong.'

F/X BURST OF STEAM AND CASTANETS
GRITPYPE THYNNE: Moriarty, men of the Royal Labour Exchange, good news. I have had talks with the Prime Minister and he has granted us a further extension of unemployment.
ORCHESTRA AND GRAMS: CHEERS

We're off, and the audience laughter spurs us on to ad libs which will eventually have to be edited out.

When the Show comes to an end, with Eccles saying: 'Well, dat's dat!' the audience leaves – some of them bewildered, the *aficionados* gleefully repeating the Bluebottle-Eccles exchanges, or the familiar catchphrase: 'And there's more where that came from.'

We sign autographs at the stage door and say our goodnights. 'See you next week, lads.' Next Sunday is already something to look forward to. Peter gives Spike a lift back to Highgate in his new American car. The electric windows go up and down as they move off. 'Ned of Wales is a pouf,' shouts Milligan as they round the corner. I blow a raspberry. 'And there's more where that came from . .' I wish there were.

20   **W**hich is the **W**ay to
the Crocodiles?

The African plain shimmered in the noonday heat, and the flies clung stubbornly to the sweat around my eyes. I could see the tail of the big cat twitching behind the clump of thorn bushes where it was lying up after the kill.

My bearer handed me the big express rifle. 'Be sure with this one, Bwana.' He seemed concerned.

I took the gun and smiled tightly. 'All right Ndoko, I'm ready.'

Our whispers must have reached the lion's ears. With a growl it slunk from its lair, crouching low as it saw us. I put the gun to my shoulder and stood firm. The lion sprang, roaring, into the air. Steadily I squeezed the trigger.

'SECOMBE!'

I was jerked back to the Lower Fourth classroom, recaptured by the acid tongue of the English master. He stood over me, thumbs hooked in his waistcoat pockets, his breath heavy with lunchtime bitter.

'Well, Secombe, dreaming again are we?'

He looked around the class for approval. The boys sniggered in anticipation.

'I'll ask you again then. What is a satire?' He rapped me heavily on the head with my ruler to emphasise each word.

My toes wriggled desperately in my black gym shoes.

'A satire, sir?'

David S. Miles, B.A., known throughout the school as Dai Laughing, nodded, ruler poised. I took a deep breath.

'A satire, sir, is a precious stone.'

The whole class crashed into laughter in time with the ruler's downward arc.

That scene was repeated endlessly in school until I perfected the technique of paying apparently riveted attention to the teacher, repeating the last few words of each of his key paragraphs, and nodding sagely at the same time. All the while, though, I was off in Africa, hunting lions or cutting my way with a panga through dense undergrowth in search of the beautiful White Queen.

I was Africa mad. Every film on the dark continent which filtered through the third re-run cinema circuit to the decrepit flea-pit which fed the dreams of our neighbourhood I saw over and over again. I would go in on the matinée and sit through until the last performance, reeling out at the end stuffed with tiger nuts and sherbert.

I was a spotty-faced Tarzan and drummed my chest with such vigour that I developed a stoop. My jungle call was so loud that it once resulted in the local policeman pedalling frantically into the park behind our house looking for a murder victim. He found only a lone ululating ten-year-old idiot half-way up a tree draped in his mother's old fur stole.

When a coloured family moved into the neighbourhood I stalked them for two weeks with a wooden spear, until my mother decided to call a halt. Anyway, they were Indians.

Africa never ceased to fascinate me and when, some years ago, I had an invitation to go on a safari, I was off like a shot to the Army & Navy Stores to be fitted for shorts and several pairs of unsoiled white duck.

Thus it was that I strode on to the verandah of my hotel in Nairobi in the freshness of an African morning, showing a full inch of leg between bottom of shorts and the top of my khaki stockings. On my head I wore a bush hat, and a pair of suede desert boots completed my white hunter ensemble.

An American couple having an early breakfast paused abruptly in mid-kedgeree. Across the hotel yard a parrot chained to a stand set up a raucous screeching. I returned to my room and changed into sports coat and flannels. If I was ready for Africa, Africa was not quite ready for me.

My spirits lightened somewhat when we headed for the Nairobi National Park, where giraffe, lion and other wild life go about their business completely disregarding the planes which roar over their heads to and from the airport a few hundred yards away. We had only just got past the barrier into the Park when a large baboon jumped on to the bonnet and performed a disgustingly human act, at the conclusion of which it bowed politely and held out its hand for a nut.

It was like that all the way. Lions rolled playfully on their backs like cats wanting to be tickled, giraffes nibbled disdainfully at the top of thorn bushes ignoring us completely, and as we left the park the baboon gave a farewell performance on the car bonnet – this time with a partner.

Disillusionment set in. Where was my Africa? The Africa of my boyhood imaginings? This was Longleat with flies.

Murchison Falls was our next stop, involving a long dusty journey into Uganda by car. After a fairly uneventful trip, during which most of the scenery was blotted out by the clouds of dust from the cars in front, we arrived some days later on the banks of the White Nile just in time to drive on to the last ferry to the camp.

I sat near the edge of the flat-bottomed boat and tried to catch a piece of floating vegetation. A passing log winked at me.

'There's a greater concentration of crocodiles here than anywhere else in Africa,' said an Army major laconically.

'Oh yes,' I said interestedly from the roof of the car.

The sun was low on the horizon when we drove off on the other side, and I decided bravely to walk the half mile or so to the camp. I had gone about three hundred yards up the track, when a man leading a small boy by the hand approached from the opposite direction. In a thick Scottish accent he enquired 'Which is the way to the crocodiles?'

Astonished, I pointed back to the river. He thanked me and walked on into the gathering dusk. 'We'll just be in time,' he said to the boy. I never saw them again.

Our short stay at Murchison was a comfortable one, and we were able to observe elephants and hippos without the slightest danger, a fact which irked me after a while. I was still in search of the real unspoiled Africa.

My chance came a few days later when I was invited to accompany a game warden on one of his regular trips in search of poachers. Our base was a permanent camp near the Uganda border with the Congo. We were to sleep in sleeping bags and really rough it. At last, I thought, this is it.

The Land-Rover we travelled in had a sticky time in the mud on the way and required my weight behind it several times. I finished up the same colour as the two native lads travelling with us. My antics in the mud appeared to amuse them no end, and I heard them refer to me several times in what I took to be Swahili.

When we got to the base camp, which consisted of one round metal hut with a straw roof and a wooden table, I mentioned to the warden that they seemed to have a name for me.

'That's good,' he said. 'If they have a special name for you it means they respect you. Try to find out what it is.'

It was getting late, so the boys built a big fire and set tin plates on the table. Beer was produced and as a Tilley lamp pumped a circle of brilliant white light around the table, dinner began.

Somewhere an animal snuffled, and flushed with beer I smiled to myself. I was Mungo Park, Livingstone and Chaka the Zulu chief all rolled into one. This was how I had always imagined it. The camp fire, the animal noises, and the convivial chat around the dinner table. Soon it will be time to slip into our sleeping bags while the native boys keep the fire going to ward off the animals, I thought.

The table was cleared and the boys, to my amazement, retired to the metal hut and shut the door.

'Time for bed,' said the warden, stretching.

I put another log on the fire.

'If you want to go to the toilet, there's one over there.' He pointed vaguely into the blackness. 'Bad form not to use it, if you know what I mean.' He tied his rifle to a pole and put out the lamp. ' 'Night,' he said wriggling into his sleeping bag. 'Watch out for hyenas.'

I sat for a while drinking beer and keeping the fire going. When the last piece of wood had gone, I looked at my watch. It was only half past eleven. Whistling tunelessly, I struggled into bed and stared uneasily about me. Out there was the whole A to Z of African wild life from Ardvaark to Zebra, and here was I lying on the ground in this open air supermarket, two hundred and twenty pounds of human flesh, fresh and ready wrapped. I fell asleep and dreamed of my happy days at school.

Three times I awoke that night to make the trip to the primitive toilet, and each time I felt that I was about to be deprived of my manhood. Hyenas are not particular in their eating habits.

Dawn was never so welcome as that day, and I greeted it like a long lost brother. I was up sluicing my naked body as the native boys emerged from their safe little hut.

One of them laughed and pointed at me. 'Tumbo Mkubwa,' he said.

I turned proudly to the game warden who was now awake and sat regarding me with some amusement.

'There, that's the name they called me before. What does it mean?'

He reached out and untied the rifle from the pole beside him, taking his time. 'Big Belly,' he said.

Somehow, it was the final indignity.

21 Busy Doing Nothing

'I'm going to do nothing today. There's an art in it you know,' I said from the bed to my wife Myra who was up and dressed.

'You're due for a degree then,' she replied with a tiny sniff of disapproval, 'It's half past nine.'

'No, what I mean My,' – I call her My and she calls me Har, except when she's mad at me, then it's Harry – 'I'm going to write a piece on doing nothing, so I'm really going to try to do nothing all day.'

'But, Harry, I'm going up to town this morning to have my hair done and then I'm going shopping with Jennifer, and somebody's got to pick up Katy from school at twelve.'

'I'm going to do nothing today except pick up Katy from school at twelve,' I amended.

It was a lovely sunny day and I lay back in a lounging chair in the garden wearing shorts, determined to relax completely. Somewhere I read that to achieve this, one has to breathe in and out slowly seven times. I was on the sixth inhalation when the phone rang. 'Let it ring,' I thought, breathing quickly again. It rang insistently whilst I pretended not to hear, at the same time wondering who it could be. My agent – no, he's in Spain; perhaps they've had an accident on the way to town. I heaved myself to my feet and headed indoors.

I picked up the phone. 'Is that Boodles Club?' said a plummy voice. We get a lot of calls for Boodles, their number must be very near ours on the dial.

'Sorry,' I said, 'wrong number.'

'I say, are you *sure* you're not Boodles?'

158

'Of course I'm bloody sure,' I slammed the receiver down savagely.

I turned to go back to the garden. The phone rang again. 'Get stuffed,' I said to the vicar.

Ten minutes and a promised church fête opening later, I was back on the lounging chair. I began the deep breathing bit again. As my belly began to rise and fall I became disgusted with myself. When I was in the army, I thought, there wasn't an ounce of fat on me.

I took a deep breath and held it. My stomach receded an inch or two. It's not all fat after all, Harry boy. Scarlet with effort, I slowly let the air out of my lungs, still holding my diaphragm in. Just a moment, I thought, I'm supposed to be doing nothing, and here I am exercising. I relaxed and the large pink hummock appeared again.

Ah, the army – that was the place for doing nothing, provided you went about it hard enough. As a clerk in a battery office I learned that by striding purposefully from the room with a piece of paper in one hand, and my eyes fixed on some distant horizon, no questions were asked about my ultimate destination, which was invariably the NAAFI.

There is the story of a private in the army who carried the paper ploy even further. He began to walk about the parade ground in Aldershot picking up pieces of paper, studying them carefully, and discarding them saying 'That's not it.' He kept this up for such a long time that he was sent to an Army mental hospital. There he continued walking around the wards and the hospital grounds searching for odd bits of paper, murmuring 'No, that's not it,' and throwing them over his shoulder.

Eventually he was taken before an Army Medical Board.

'I'm afraid we're going to have to let you go on mental grounds,' said the examining officer as he made out a discharge certificate.

He handed it to the private who examined it carefully and shouted 'That's it!'

Good God, I must have dropped off. I looked at my watch – nearly ten to twelve. No time to change, I'd have to fetch Katy as I was. There was a waterproof golfing jacket in the garage and I slipped it on over my shorts.

I arrived at the school with two minutes to spare, parked the car and found that I had to stand uneasily with a group of mothers waiting for the kids to come out. I pretended a great interest in a gold fish pond, whistling insanely to the fish, aware all the time that my eccentric garb was causing some amusement. Katy came out, took one look at me and yelled, "Daddy's got no trousers on.' I picked her up and ran with her to the car.

She chattered all the way home. 'Justin put a live worm in my hair,' she complained, 'and Sarah Jane was sick.' Mariella had apparently drawn a house upside down, Martin had fallen out of a tree and was dead, and Christina was going to marry silly old Neil. As I listened, I wondered what ever had happened to the Gwyneths and Llewellyns and Gladyses and Freds of my school days. I remembered the blurred photographs taken featuring a slate reading 'Class II 1927' held by the brightest boy in the class, and me fifth from the left in the third row, partly obscured by a boy with his head shaved because of ringworm.

Back home again, I gave Katy her lunch and resumed the prone position in the garden. Now, where was I, I thought – doing nothing, of course. I fell back, eyes glazing, smiling to myself. Katy sat on my chest. 'That's my chair,' she claimed.

'It's not, it's mine,' I felt nearer to the classroom photographs.

She shifted her weight on to my stomach and started jumping up and down on it.

'All right, all right,' I said, 'have it.'

I went across to the garden shed to get another chair. It was dark in there and I scraped my bare shin against the mower.

'Bloody hell,' I shouted, hopping about.

'Bloody hell! Bloody hell!' Katy cried in delight. She loves swear words, and three months in Australia where I made a film earlier in the year, had given her a vocabulary which made us blanch whenever we had visitors.

With a great effort I stifled my sobs and set out the other chair.

The dogs started to bark.

'The dogs are barking,' said Katy.

'I know, I can hear,' I shouted.

She started to cry. 'You shouted at me.'

'I'm sorry, love,' I picked her up to cuddle her.

'I'll tell Mummy you swore at me,' she said.

'I didn't swear at you, I swore because I hurt my leg.'

'Is it bleeding? Let me see.' Katy loves to see a drop of blood. She is either going to be a doctor or a lady butcher.

'It's stopped bleeding. Jump up and down to make it start again.'

Anything for a quiet life I thought, jumping around and making funny noises to make her laugh.

'Good old Harry boy,' shouted a voice from the garden gate. It was the baker's roundsman fending off our two boxers, popularly known as the burglars' friends, who were trying to lick him to death. 'Doing a bit of dancing in your next TV show then?'

'Bugger off,' said Katy.

'Charming,' said the breadman, leaving in a huff.

'That's very naughty,' I said.

'Then why are you laughing?'

I limped back to my chair and lay down. 'Try contemplating your navel,' I said to myself. I looked down – in this position I'd need a periscope.

The door bell rang. A young lad stood outside.

'Your dogs have got out,' he said. 'They've got a lady with a poodle trapped up against the fence.' Our boxers are very docile with people, but with other dogs they are villainous. I ran round the corner and dragged them away with profuse apologies to the poodle's owner. She was very upset at first, but I managed to mollify her by offering to open a chapel bazaar. Fortunately she did not seem to know who I was. I locked the dogs in the laundry room and staggered back into the garden. Katy now had both chairs upside down and was playing house, and nothing would induce her to give one up.

'I'm supposed to be doing nothing,' I wailed.

'Well go and do it somewhere else,' she said with four-year-old logic.

I was saved from what could have been a long tearful struggle – on my part – by the arrival of my wife and eldest daughter.

'Have a nice time doing nothing?' they asked.

'It's a lost art as far as I'm concerned,' I said, 'I'm going upstairs for a kip.'

22 Middle-aged Man and the Sea

I have always been fascinated by fish, with or without chips. A lot of my time as a schoolboy in Swansea was spent watching the trawlers unloading their glittering catches at the dockside; the slabs of fishmongers' shops draw me like a magnet; Jacques Cousteau on television is an irresistible attraction, and I even bought the house in which I am now living because it had the largest tropical fish tank in South London. Unfortunately it was in the room where I rehearse my singing and an aria or two used to send the Angel Fish leaping out of the water. Eventually I gave the fish away on humanitarian grounds, with the exception of an apparently deaf Catfish which died of natural causes during a cold spell.

It is small wonder then that when my horizons began to open up I was eager to emulate Hemingway's *Old Man and the Sea*. I could see the big fish jumping high in the air, shaking the hook from side to side in a frantic effort to get free, whilst I sat firmly strapped in my chair hauling it inexorably towards the waiting gaff, exultant in victory and yet sad for the death of a brave adversary. 'Vaya con Dios' I would say, patting the dying fish.

But all my real-life experiences have never been like that. I have fished the waters of the Caribbean, the Coral Sea and the South Pacific, yet as a big game fisherman I am somewhere near the bottom of the fourth division and due for imminent relegation. In Acapulco – where the Sailfish and Black Marlin are of legendary size and everybody who goes out fishing comes back with something to show for it – when it came to my turn to take the chair I was being sick over the side. Something extremely large and vicious once took bait, hook, line and rod from me when fishing off Montego Bay. It was either a shark or a Russian submarine.

I once went fishing with an eccentric retired army officer on the Great Barrier Reef. We had been out six hours without success when he shouted 'Strike!' as the line screamed away. He pushed me into the chair and I began hauling away frantically, my heart pounding and the Foster's lager burning in my throat.

'It's a Marlin,' he said, jumping up and down and making the boat rock from side to side. I reeled in grimly.

I made one last desperate haul on the rod and up came the hook and away went a permanently smiling Marlin. My companion threw down the gaff, saying nothing as he went forward to start the engine. We made a U turn and headed back for the mainland at full speed, the lines streaming out behind us with the baited hooks a foot above our wake.

'What are we after now?' I asked lamely.

'Bloody Flying Fish,' he said without looking round.

My most recent fishing expedition was off Barbados last Christmas. We were staying, my family and I, at a hotel on that little gem of an island, and I hired a boat big enough to take us all. At eight o'clock I mustered my wife and progeny on the beach to await the launch. We had only been standing there long enough for my six-year-old daughter, Katy, to throw my eleven-year-old son David's book of horror stories into the sea to be rescued by her fifty-two-year-old father, when my twenty-four-year-old daughter, Jennifer, and my twenty-year-old son, Andrew, both pointed out to sea at a fast approaching cabin cruiser of surprising elegance and size. 'That's nice,' remarked Myra, my fortyish wife.

A smart dinghy buzzed towards the beach piloted by a

natty gent who stepped nimbly ashore and approached our suitably impressed group.

'Mrs Goldsmith's party?' he enquired.

'Over here!' cried a large American lady wearing yachting gear from behind us.

'Oh!' we said collectively, and Katy threw David's book into the water again.

Eventually we found ourselves aboard a smaller and less elegant fishing boat, but one which was fully equipped for the job. The skipper, a jolly person of a build not unlike my own, made us welcome as we headed for the deep blue water beyond the reef. We arranged ourselves around the boat – my wife and Jennifer found places in which to tan themselves, Katy and David sat in the fishing chairs and Andrew and I sat on the stern looking for any sudden flurry of flying fish, a sure sign of big fish in the area.

'This is the life,' I said removing my shirt and sun hat.

'You'll get burnt again,' said Myra.

'Nonsense,' I said, 'I've taken two sunburn prevention tablets.'

She lay back again. 'We'll see,' she said.

We trolled our lines for an hour, following the coastline.

'How about a drink?' said the skipper.

'Too early,' said Myra, knowing me.

'It may be half past nine here, but it's half past one in London,' I laughed.

Soon Andy, Jennifer and I were drinking our rum and cokes while Myra and the kids contented themselves with lemonade.

'What fish might we catch?' I asked the captain.

'Spanish Mackerel, perhaps, Wahoo or Kingfish, Barracuda, Dolphin . . .'

Katy sat up. 'You're not going to catch a Dolphin,' she cried. 'They're lovely. Flipper's a Dolphin.'

David looked up from his sodden book. 'The Dolphin is

an active pelagic spiny-finned fish constituting a genus cory-
phaena,' he quoted accurately. 'Flipper is a Porpoise.'

'No he's not!' yelled Katy and threw his book into the
sea for the last time.

'I'd finished it anyway,' he said sticking out his tongue.

This isn't Hemingway, I thought, it's A.A. Milne.

Time passed quickly enough with the rum and coke
flowing freely, and after I had conducted the family choir
in 'The Lord's My Shepherd' for the fourth time, with
Jennifer getting gradually weaker on the descant, I got up
to make my third trip to the tiny toilet.

'You'll be sorry,' said Myra squinting up at me as I
passed her. I laughed indulgently.

I had just locked myself in the loo when I heard
'STRIKE!' from the captain and confused shouts and
screams from the others. I tried to open the bolt on the
door and snagged my thumb rather badly. Katy banged on
the door screaming 'Andy's killing Flipper!' I banged back
shouting 'I can't get out. Tell your mother!'

By the time I had forced the door, leaking blood from my
thumb as I did so, it was all over and Andrew had landed
a 35-pound Wahoo – modest enough for these waters, but
still bigger than anything I had ever managed to catch. We
had drinks all round again and the boat circled looking for
another victim. It never came, and when we landed later
with the catch I stood in the background nursing my injured
thumb as Andy posed with the Wahoo.

That night Myra had to send for the doctor. 'What's
wrong with him?' he asked as he came in.

'Rum, sun and thumb,' she said. 'And a touch of the
Hemmingways.'

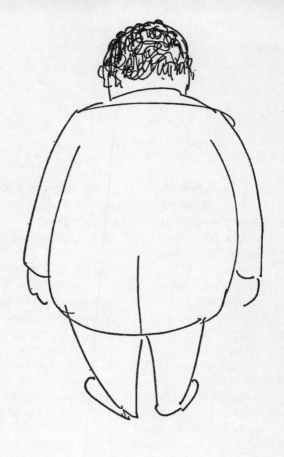

23 Goon for Lunch—Back at Ten

The phone rang at home. 'How would you like to go to the finest restaurant in France for lunch and come back the same day, all expenses paid?' asked William Davis editor of *Punch*. 'Just give me five minutes to pack my knife, fork and spoon,' I said.

And so Harry Secombe, the oldest cub reporter in the world, boarded an Air France plane at 9.20 in the morning bound for Lyons and La Pyramide Restaurant, one of the few in France to which Michelin gives three stars and which resounds to the refined chomping of the most expensive choppers in the whole of Europe.

Sitting back in my seat, I allowed myself a brief reverie of memorable meals I had partaken of in the past. I remembered the bread pudding we used to have for afters in the army in Aldershot in 1941. Our new Sergeant Cook vowed that we would have bread pudding at every meal until we stopped wasting bread. I began to acquire a taste for it and as the weeks went by I wasted so much bread that I was put on a charge.

I remembered a summer's night in Bert's Café near the Slips, Swansea, where I proposed to Myra over tea and slightly stale doughnuts. I had three to her one, saying 'Marry me and one day we will be eating champagne and caviar'. 'That's right, love,' she said without conviction as she paid the bill.

Upon reflection I began to wonder if I was the right man for the job. Head waiters, particularly on the continent, single me out for special inattention. Just as a horse knows immediately and instinctively when its rider is an idiot, so a head waiter greets my entrance to a restaurant with a knowing aside to his assistants, 'Nous avons a right one here'.

He usually lets me simmer at the table until I begin to believe the story of the head waiter who died and had inscribed on his tombstone 'At last God caught his eye'. Then when I am considered to be just about on the boil he comes along and whisks me with the menu, stirring briskly, talks fast kitchen Italian to taste, until my mind approaches the consistency of smooth paste and I find myself ordering the most expensive dish he has to offer, which upon close inspection turns out to be a kind of rissole.

On arrival, a car complete with young chauffeur awaited me. 'Aah, la puissance de Punch,' I exclaimed. He smiled incomprehendingly. After a few miles my stock French phrases ran out. 'Meubles,' I said desperately as we passed a furniture shop. 'Oui,' he said, vaguely surprised. A quarter of a mile of silence later I said 'Boulangerie'. He nodded uncomfortably. After I had idiotically pointed out a hospital, a paper shop and a funeral parlour he said 'I learn English. If Monsieur would like to speak with me it would be good for my study.' I accepted with relief. 'Blimey, I felt a right twit,' I said. He looked uncomfortable. We rode on in silence. Then, 'Pharmacy,' he said, indicating a chemist shop.

The drive out to Vienne, where the restaurant is situated, takes about 45 minutes. The weather was sunny and I watched the glorious scenery flash past with a mounting feeling of excitement. It seemed no time before we arrived at Vienne, which is a very ancient town where Pontius Pilate is supposed to have ended his days. From what I saw of it, it was much too good for him.

We came at last to my gastronomic mecca as we rounded the four-fronted arch surmounted by a pyramid from which the restaurant takes its name. Founded in 1920 by Monsieur

Fernand Point, it has become over the years a place of pilgrimage for the world's top gourmets.

The restaurant garden was green and lovely, but with one unusual feature, there were empty bottles stuck all over the fruit trees. This perplexed me somewhat. Inside the restaurant a young waiter wearing a long white apron seemed to know that I was the gentleman from England. There was an atmosphere of deceptive homely provincial charm about the place. The room had a low ceiling with wood panelled walls, green velvet curtains at the windows, and three rows of tables ran its whole length. A large oval table stood before the wooden screen at the kitchen end of the restaurant. On it were piles of gleaming cutlery and a huge carved wooden bowl containing enough lemons for a whole football season of half time refreshments.

The place wasn't very full. The dress of the clientele was in the main casual, and although the chatter was relaxed and uninhibited, one could hear above everything the faint rustle of crisp 100 franc notes. This was obviously not luncheon voucher territory. But why, I asked myself, should they hang bottles on trees in the garden? I was placed at a table in the right-hand corner of the room and as I sat down I took out a small note book and put it in front of me, determined to record this momentous meal course by course.

The head waiter was a short, red-faced jolly little man who introduced himself as Monsieur Vincent and handed me a large menu before bustling away. On the front of the menu was the Pyramide motif which, incidentally, was repeated throughout the restaurant. Even the butter on each table was moulded in its shape. I viewed the menu with reverence and was faced with an agonising choice of classic French dishes written in longhand. I decided to let the Maitre D'Hotel choose for me. 'Je suis dans vos mains,' I said. He winced a little then smiled. 'Permettez-moi, monsieur,' was his reply as he whipped the menu away. Remembering my past experiences with head waiters I had a sudden vision of rissoles.

The long crusty bread roll looked very inviting and as I sank my teeth into it I made a note on my pad. 'Long crusty bread roll,' I wrote. The wine list arrived along with the wine waiter in a green baize apron. I mention them in that order because of the size of the wine list. It was enormous and rather than spend a long time holding it I asked the wine waiter to recommend a half bottle of white and a half bottle of red. He came back with an unlabelled white wine in a bucket. When I asked him the name I was unable to understand what he said, so not wanting to seem impolite I nodded sagely. 'Vin blanc' I jotted on my pad.

'*Brioche de foie gras,*' said the waiter as he laid the first course before me. I tabulated its description for posterity 'Square slice of sweet bread with round piece of pâté in the middle – very nice.' I ate it quickly, not having had any breakfast. For no reason at all I worried again about the bottles on the trees.

Very soon the waiter was back with a second course. '*Mousse de fruite périgueuse,*' he announced. I picked up my fork and spoon and demolished it in seconds. 'Cylindrical shaped mousse with black gritty bits in the sauce' was my entry. I took a quick swill of wine and sat back sweating slightly. Monsieur Vincent came across to the table. 'Mange doucement, monsieur,' he admonished kindly. I had the grace to blush and resolved to treat the next course with more delicacy.

Turbot au champagne was almost immediately in front of me. The service throughout being prompt and impeccable. Now this was really delicious. Probably the best fish course I have ever tasted. I lingered over the sauce, surreptitiously dipping the remains of my roll in it and washing the whole lot down with great drafts of the white wine. 'Smashing – not a bone in it,' was my written comment.

The waiters then entered bearing a huge serving dish called, I believe, a *torpilleure*, on which were two smaller silver dishes and between them a bowl containing two roses. This course turned out to be *Caneton Nantais au Poire Vert*. It was duck cooked in a rich sauce with a side plate of thinly sliced potatoes done in a kind of omelette. The wine waiter brought along a bottle of Côte Rotie, 1964. He poured out a little for me to taste. I made a great business of rolling the wine around my tongue with my eyes shut. 'A very good year for corks,' I quipped. 'Pardon, monsieur?' his eyes narrowed a little. 'Très bien,' I said hastily, starting to tackle the duck. I was beginning to breathe heavily by this time and although I ate the omelette I left some of the duck. The wine was having an effect on my notes too. 'Duck' was all I managed to write, relying on my taste buds to be the espouser of lost courses.

Another glass of wine and along came the cheese. Excellent it was and to make sure of the name I got the waiter to put it down for me. 'Coulommiers' was what he wrote. I hoped it wasn't a rude comment. The next courses are a little mixed in my mind. Did I really have *Gateau Marjolaine* followed by fresh strawberries and cream and a sorbet? There are traces on my waistcoat to prove that I must have.

My eyes were beginning to close as Monsieur Vincent approached with a bottle of liqueur containing a fully grown pear. He insisted that I should taste some with my coffee. I wondered vaguely how the pear got inside, until a very French looking couple at the next table, who turned out to be very English, explained how it was done. They put the neck of the bottle over a bud on the pear tree and let it grow inside, then when the pear is ripe they remove the bottle from the tree and fill it up with pear brandy. 'Of course, how simple,' I beamed around the room, replete and happy with the best meal I had ever had safely under my belt and the mystery solved. The bill came and went without removing the smile from my face and I insisted on shaking hands with all the staff. 'Vive le Common Market,' I said. 'Oui,' was the qualified reply.

I was still smiling when I got home at ten that night. 'Well was it worth the trip?' asked my wife, fresh from cooking beefburgers for the kids' supper. 'Best meal I've ever had,' I said, 'In a restaurant that is,' I added quickly seeing her expression. 'Bet they couldn't make a proper cup of tea,' she said placing one before me. 'They certainly couldn't,' I said, 'but they can grow pears in bottles.' 'You've been drinking,' she said.